Creative Suet Cookery

ROZ DENNY

Published by Martin Books
8 Market Passage, Cambridge CB2 3PF
in association with RHM Foods Ltd
10 Victoria Road, London NW10 6NU

First published 1980
© RHM Foods Ltd and Roz Denny 1980
ISBN 0 85941 144 3

Featured on the cover picture are Cumberland pudding
(p. 57), Date 'n nutty doughnuts (p. 66), Pork terrine en
croûte (p. 33).

Contents

Introducing Suet

Suet is, perhaps, the purest, most natural fat known to us. Even in its convenient form, ready shredded, it has merely been clarified, then lightly coated in fine wheat flour. This process was used by many old cooks in Regency and Victorian times and cleverly imitated by an enterprising Frenchman, Gabriel Hugon, who set up the first Atora factory in 1893 in Manchester.

Although for many years associated with long, slow boiling, suet can form the basis of many quick cooking main meals and snacks that require around half an hour to cook. If you add that to the short preparation time (it needs merely to be mixed with other ingredients – the original 'all in one' method), then suet must surely be an essential ingredient in today's food cupboard.

WHAT IS SUET?

Suet is the hard fat found around the kidneys in all animals, including Man, as a protective coating. Atora suet is pure beef suet, the least flavoured and therefore most adaptable. In its natural form, it needs to be cleansed of any membranes or tissue, grated or finely chopped and then used quite quickly before it starts to go rancid. Ready shredded suet is the same product, but purified and easy to use straight from the packet – there are no additives or preservatives and yet it will keep for up to a year in a store cupboard without refrigeration.

Suet has been used for centuries in cooking as it was often the most available and cheapest fat. Old recipes abound with interesting and delicious ways of using suet from puddings and pies to rich moist stuffings and even in hot rice puddings and milky drinks. An Atora Cook Book of 1933 gives 'A Splendid Home Remedy' of a spoonful of Atora in a hot milky bedtime drink which it says 'is very soothing and beneficial in the case of a cough and sore throat.'

Finally, on a dietary note, suet compares favourably with other fats, such as butter, and like them is a good source of concentrated energy, with around nine calories in every gram. This makes it a good food for those with high energy needs and small appetites, such as children, or those with physically demanding jobs. Fat also plays another major role in our diet – it has what is termed a high satiety value, that is, it makes food remain longer in the stomach, so one does not become hungry as quickly.

Note on measurements
Whilst the dual system of weighing and measuring still exists in this country it is necessary to list both in the recipes. To minimise the confusion, I have arranged quantities in two columns – metric on the left and imperial on the right.

The dual units are not exact conversions, but workable alternatives according to equipment and foods sold. So, for example, although 450 g is nearer 1 lb than 500 g, it would not be sold as that and the difference is minimal. Also, to keep to exact proportions of ingredients, e.g. half suet to flour, it has been necessary to use different equivalents on occasions.

For maximum success, do not mix the two systems, stick to either metric or imperial.

Basic Recipes and Information

BASIC SUET RECIPES

The normal rule of thumb is to use half suet to flour (usually self-raising) and/or breadcrumbs. It's that simple.

To make it simpler still, if you do not want to get the scales out allow 2 × 15 ml spoons/2 tablespoons of flour to each 15 ml spoon/tablespoon of suet. Mix in enough cold water to form a stiff dough, normally just under a 15 ml spoon/tablespoon for each 25 g/1 oz flour.

Quick Shortcut Pastry

This is ideal pastry for new cooks, bachelors and those who feel they will never master the art of pastry making! It's so easy because there is no need to rub in. Using the formula above, measure 100 g/4 oz of self-raising flour into a bowl, add 50 g/2 oz shredded suet, season to taste and mix to a firm dough with a beaten egg, plus cold water or milk if necessary. Roll out on a lightly floured surface to about 5 mm/¼ in. thick, the thickness of two 10p coins.

Always roll in one direction only, in short, light strokes, normally away from you, giving the pastry a quarter turn to the left after every roll, that way you will keep a nice round shape, although if you want a square or oblong shape you don't need to turn so often.

To place the pastry in position over a pie dish, lift it gently over the rolling pin, otherwise you could stretch it, with the result that it will shrink back when cooked.

Hint If you add a 5 ml spoon/1 teaspoon baking powder to the self-raising flour the pastry becomes so light it's like a cheat's flaky pastry.

Light-as-a-feather Dumplings

As with the pastry, don't use too much water in the making. Always use sifted self-raising flour, or a 5 ml spoon/1 teaspoon of fresh baking powder to each 100 g/ 4 oz plain flour, and a good pinch of salt. Make up the same basic formula of half suet to flour – a 100 g/4 oz mixture of flour will give you about eight uncooked dumplings the size of fresh apricots. Drop them into salted *simmering* water or stock, cover and cook for 20 minutes. If they break up it is because the simmer is not gentle enough. Don't put in too many at one time, otherwise they will all swell up and join together.

Dumplings are normally cooked on top of a stew or hot pot, but you can also cook them on their own, as above. They are ideal for adding flavours to, depending on what you intend to serve them with. Try adding the grated rind of half a lemon, or a 5 ml spoon/1 teaspoon of dried herbs, or a little grated cheese, such as Parmesan or Cheddar.

Moist and Rich Stuffings

The other traditional use for shredded suet is in wonderful flavoursome stuffings and making up is very simple. I always keep a box of fresh white and brown breadcrumbs in the freezer – they don't stick fast together and are easy to weigh out. Again, half suet to breadcrumbs is the formula with seasonings, and binding with a beaten egg, about one size 3 egg to each 100 g/4 oz breadcrumbs. For flavours, a grated onion is always a good base, plus a little crushed garlic, if liked. Then make up your own additional flavourings according to the meat or vegetable to be stuffed.

Some suggested flavourings Grated lemon or orange rind, lots of fresh chopped herbs or half quantity of dried, chopped walnuts or almonds, grated apple, grated cheese, anchovy essence, chopped bacon or ham, curry powder, chopped mushrooms, chopped apricots, chopped chestnuts and, for rich stuffings, one 15 ml spoon/1 tablespoon or two of sherry or vermouth.

See also stuffings in Festive Favourites on page 94.

Flaky Pastry

A suet flaky pastry is easily made as there is no need to rub in any fat at the start. Instead, mix in some shredded suet and then proceed as normal. One of the secrets of success is to make sure that your edges are as straight as possible so that when you fold the dough, the portions are equal. Coax gently with your hands if necessary, and always turn in one direction only, normally anti-clockwise.

250 g	plain flour (*not* self-raising)	8 oz
	pinch of salt	
90 g	shredded suet	3 oz
15 ml spoon	lemon juice	1 tablespoon
	iced cold water, to mix	
90 g	butter, slightly creamed	3 oz

Method

1 Sift the flour and salt together, then stir in the suet. Mix to a firm dough with the lemon juice and water.

2 Cream the butter slightly and divide into three.

3 Roll out the dough and try to keep the edges as straight as possible.

4 Using a small palette or table knife, dot one third of the butter as evenly as possible over two thirds of the pastry to within 1 cm/½ in. of the edge.

5 Fold the remaining unbuttered third up onto the centre third, then fold the top third over that. Press all edges together firmly, but gently with the sides of your hands. Give a quarter turn to the left and using as little extra flour as possible, roll out to a neat rectangle about 5 mm/¼ in. thick.

6 Dot with the next third of butter and repeat the process, then again with the last third, always turning in the same direction.

7 Fold the pastry into three again, cover with foil or cling film and leave to rest in the fridge or larder for at least an hour.

8 Bake in a hot oven at 200–220°C/400–425°F/Gas Mark 6–7.

Uses for flaky pastry

Use for sweet and savoury dishes, especially meat and fruit pies, or, roll out to 10 cm/4 in. squares and use to make turnovers, such as apple, jam or mincemeat. Alternatively, make up savoury fillings like tuna and chopped hard boiled egg binding with some white sauce if serving hot, or mayonnaise if cold. Leftover mince, spiced up with some curry powder will make a quick variation of the Indian 'turnovers' called samozas.

Sausage rolls (picture on page 87)

Use a good quality sausage meat. Roll out the pastry into a long oblong, roll the sausage meat to an equal length and place down one side. Damp the edges, fold over the other side, seal and crimp with the prongs of a fork. Cut slits down the centre with a sharp knife or kitchen scissors, cut into required lengths – bite size or normal – glaze with a little milk or beaten egg and bake for 20–25 minutes at 200°C/400°F/Gas Mark 6 until golden.

Vol-au-vents

Roll out the pastry to 1 cm/½ in. thick and using a 6.5 cm/2½ in. cutter, press out as many rounds as possible. Using a smaller round cutter, or bottle top, about 3 cm/1½ in., press half way through the rounds. Glaze and bake at 220°C/425°F/Gas Mark 7 for about 15 minutes until risen and crisp. With a sharp knife, remove the tops and reserve, scoop out any soggy pastry and put the bottoms back into the oven to dry out for about 5 minutes.

Fill with savoury, flavoursome fillings such as chicken, mushroom, prawn, ham or tuna, using a well seasoned thick white sauce as a base. Finally, replace the tops and serve hot or cold.

Choux Pastry

Shredded suet can even be used to make choux buns, although these are more suited to hot savoury fillings such as the smoked haddock filling on page 48, or those for vol-au-vents above.

Choux buns with tuna and egg filling, Vol-au-vents with chicken and prawn filling, Noughts and crosses (p. 84)

50 g	shredded suet	2 oz
150 ml	water	¼ pint
50 g	plain flour (*not* self-raising)	2 oz
	pinch of salt	
2	eggs, size 2, well beaten	2

Method

1 Put the suet and water in a medium-size pan and heat slowly until all the suet has melted, then bring to the boil.

2 Remove from the heat and immediately tip in the flour and salt. With a wooden spoon, beat hard until it forms a large, soft but firm, ball of dough which leaves the side of the pan. Warning – it looks awful at first!

3 Allow to cool for a few minutes then add the beaten eggs, a little at a time, mixing in thoroughly until the mixture is a firm dropping consistency, i.e. it will drop from a wooden spoon if jerked. You may not need all the egg.

4 Put into a piping bag with a large plain nozzle, 1 cm/½ in. round. Pipe out even blobs, the size of a 50p piece, on a greased and wet baking sheet, leaving enough room for expansion. The water helps the buns to rise. If you do not have a piping bag, then just spoon the mixture onto the sheet.

5 Bake at 220°C/425°F/Gas Mark 7 for about 25 minutes until golden and puffed up, or according to your recipe. Remove from the heat, slit one side open and return to the oven for about 5 minutes for the insides to dry out.

MAKING PERFECT PIES

Baking Blind

Line the base of a flan dish or ring on a baking sheet, taking care not to stretch the pastry. Hold a sharp knife at an angle and cut the pastry away evenly. Prick the base with a fork and line with either greaseproof paper and baking beans (a mixture of old pearl barley, rice, dried peas, etc.) or foil.

Bake, normally at 200°C/400°F/Gas Mark 6 for a total of 15 minutes, removing the paper or foil and beans after 10 minutes. The pastry should look just cooked, if it does not, then return it for a few minutes more.

Covering Pies

* Edge pie dishes first with strips of pastry trimmings, then damp with water, milk or glaze. Gently lift the pastry onto the pie filling with a rolling pin. Press lightly into place.
* For neatly trimmed edges, hold the dish up with your left hand and with a sharp knife pointing away from you, cut the overlap off at right angles.
* For simple crimping, press with the prongs of a fork or the end of a table knife, otherwise *knock up* by pressing down on the edge with your left finger and cutting lightly and quickly into the edge with a knife.
* For a truly professional finish, make a pinch on the knocked up edge and cut into it at right angles.
* A glaze of beaten egg gives the best golden brown, otherwise use milk.

Simple and Effective Decorations

* Use trimmings, re-roll to a 5 mm/¼ in. thickness.
* For leaves, cut into strips according to the width of the leaves, normally 1 cm/½ in. thick. Cut into diamonds then mark out 'veins' with a sharp knife. Twist when fixing onto the pie.
* For plaits, as on the Terrine en Croûte in our cover picture, make long thin strips and plait together.
* For tassels, cut out a strip 15 × 2.5 cm/6 × 1 in. Make cuts along the strip to within 5 mm/¼ in. of one edge. Roll up loosely, hold the uncut edge and gently fold the cut strips down over it. Fix over the central hole in a pie.
* For fancy shapes, simply stamp out pastry with small aspic cutters, very small scone cutters, or a bottle top.
* For a lattice top, as on the Old English Treacle Tart on page 50, cut out long 1 cm/½ in. strips and arrange in a criss cross, twisting and/or weaving depending on your time and patience.

* Glaze all decorations well. On sweet pies, use an egg white glaze and sprinkle with caster sugar.

MAKING PERFECT PUDDINGS

Lining a Pudding Basin with Suet Pastry
As a rough guide, you need to roll your pastry out to a circle the same diameter as the two sides and base added together, allowing for a 5 mm/¼ in. thickness. Cut out a quarter and reserve for the lid. Make a cone shape with the remaining three quarters and fit into a greased pudding basin. Mould *gently* into shape, pressing and pulling as necessary and allowing sufficient overhang at the top. Knead the remaining quarter and re-roll to a circle large enough to fit the top. Fill with your chosen mixture, place the lid on top, dampen the overhanging edges and press together to seal. Trim away the excess pastry and cover (see below). Cook immediately.

Covering Pudding Basins
Use greased greaseproof paper, aluminium foil or, if you have one tucked away, a traditional linen pudding cloth, although clean old sheeting will do just as well. The advantage of the old pudding cloths was that they could be washed out and re-used time and time again.

Pleat the greaseproof paper, foil or cloth once to allow the pudding to rise. If using foil, secure by turning the edges under with one hand whilst supporting the top with the other. It may look awkward at first, but with a bit of practice it soon becomes a simple operation and a lot easier than struggling with string. If you want to use string though, choose cotton thread not nylon.

If your pan is a bit small to allow you to take the basin out easily, then make a long treble thickness of foil and sit the basin on that, with the edges hanging over the pan. Or, if using string, make a handle of string over the top.

Making a Roly-poly
Roll out to a large rectangle, 5 mm/¼ in. thick – this is usually about 25 × 20 cm/10 × 8 in. Spread the filling or

jam to within 1 cm/½ in. of the edges. Roll up firmly but not too tight and trim the edges to neaten. Place join side down on greased greaseproof paper, then follow steps below if boiling, or if baking glaze with an egg or milk and place on a baking sheet.

Covering Roly-polys

Wrap loosely, but still quite firmly in greased grease-proof paper, allowing room for expansion but holding the shape in. Overwrap with a double thickness of foil and press and fold the ends and joins together. That should be sufficient to keep the water out but let the steam in. Sit on an old china household plate with enough water to come halfway up the roll. If using a pudding cloth, tie the ends with string.

Boiling and Steaming Puddings and Roly-polys

You'll need either a large pan with a well fitting lid, or a steamer with a lid. For the latter, there is no need to buy a special pan and steamer set, the steamer can often be bought on its own with three ridges on the base to fit the most popular sizes of saucepan. If you have a fish kettle with a lift out trivet, then that, too, is super for cooking puddings and roly-polys – in fact you can do two or three at once.

Whatever method you use, the water must at all times be actually boiling from the moment you put the pudding in, and that includes any water added to top up. If it is not boiling you could get a heavy pudding.

If boiling, place the basin on an old saucer in case it cracks. Pour in enough boiling water to come half way up the sides of the basin and adjust the heat to a medium boil rather than a simmer. Cover with a well fitting lid. If it is not a good fit, cover first with greaseproof or foil, that way you'll cut down on evaporation and only have to top up once or twice with water. I find it useful to carry round a kitchen timer to remind me to check the water level every half hour or so.

Take care when removing the pan lid and pudding, and use an oven cloth as steam can scald quite badly.

Allow puddings to stand for a few minutes before

turning out and run a knife around the sides of the basin before doing so. One tip I picked up from the Atora Kitchens was to put a disc of buttered paper on the bottom of the basin for puddings without jam or syrup in the base, then they just plopped out onto the serving dish without leaving any mixture behind. Also, never fill a basin more than two thirds full of mixture, to allow for expansion.

PRESSURE COOKER PUDDINGS

Pressure cooking is a sort of 'super steaming' process and a great time saver when it comes to cooking suet puddings. Below are some basic guidelines but *you would do well to consult your instruction manual first* as there are two main types of cooker, those with an overall pressure of 7½ lb and the more conventional cooker with three weights of 15, 10 and 5 lb. For steamed puddings use the 5 lb (low) weight in this type of cooker.

1 Add at least 750 ml/1½ pints of boiling water to the pan, more for longer cooking times. Place the trivet rim side down on the base, or the basket, depending on the model.

2 The pudding will need 15 minutes conventional steaming, covered but without the weights.

3 After steaming, bring to pressure with weights and cook 7½ lb ones for a third of the conventional time, excluding the initial steaming, e.g. if a recipe states 1½ hours, pressure cook for half an hour. For 5 lb (low) weights follow this chart:

Given recipe time	=	Steaming	+	Pressure cooking
30 minutes		5 minutes		10 minutes
1 hour		15 minutes		25 minutes
2–3 hours		20 minutes		50–60 minutes

4 Reduce the pressure slowly, by removing the pan carefully from the heat and wait for about 15 minutes. The lid can be lifted when the weight gives just a gentle hiss when removed.

MICROWAVE PUDDINGS AND ROLY-POLYS

With the ease with which suet mixtures can be prepared and the speed at which microwave ovens can cook, the serving of a wholesome, delicious pudding or roly-poly becomes a simple operation of about quarter of an hour from store cupboard to table. And the result is very good!

It is rather difficult to offer specific cooking times as not only do models differ between manufacturers (just like conventional gas and electric cookers) but they also operate at different power levels which in turn affects the rate at which the same dish can cook in different ovens.

However, you might like to try the following guide-lines which are the result of testwork carried out on a fairly typical domestic microwave oven operating at 700 watts power level, using the full and defrost controls only. If your own instruction booklet gives specific instructions for suet mixtures, then naturally follow those instead.

* Always use non-metal containers such as household china or heat-resistant glass. Cover puddings with cling-film and pierce a hole in the top to allow the steam to escape. If you wish to obtain a traditional steamed pudding texture, then place a cup of water in the oven with the pudding basin.
* Wrap roly-polys in greased greaseproof paper allowing room for expansion. You may also need to unwrap them halfway through the cooking time to help the top cook properly.
* Unless you have a special microwave turntable you will need to turn the dish every couple of minutes or so to prevent heat spots forming.
* Remember, a microwave oven does not brown food unless there is a special browning unit incorporated in it, and whilst this may not matter for some dishes you may want a nice golden brown colour on others such as a roly-poly or treacle pudding. If this is the case, then simply use darker ingredients, such as brown sugar and wholemeal flour.

Microwave Cooking Times for Typical Suet Mixtures

Filled puddings e.g. steak and kidney or apple, where the basin is lined with suet pastry and the filling, if meat, is pre-cooked.

Size of basin, 0.85–1.1 litre/1½–2 pint.

Total cooking time – 8 minutes on full power. Turn every 2 minutes. Stand for 2 minutes before serving.

'Steamed' puddings e.g. jam, syrup or spotted dick types.

Size of basin, 0.85–1.1 litre/1½–2 pint.

Total cooking time is 6 minutes on full power. Turn every 1½ minutes. Stand for 2 minutes before serving.

Roly-polys using 150 g/6 oz flour in pastry.

Total cooking time is 8 minutes on full power. Turn every 2 minutes. Unwrap after 4 minutes if in grease-proof paper to allow top to cook evenly. Stand for 2 minutes before serving.

Dumplings cooked in lightly salted water or a stew.

Total cooking time is 20 minutes on defrost power, turning every 5 minutes. Full power is not suitable as it causes the water to boil and the dumplings to break up.

Christmas puddings raw mixture in 0.85–1.1 litre/1½–2 pint basins.

Total cooking time is 10 minutes on full power, but allow to stand 3 minutes half way through cooking, then stand for 20 minutes before serving.

SLOW COOKING DUMPLINGS AND PUDDINGS

At the other end of the scale, a slow cooker can also be used to cook various suet dishes, namely dumplings, puddings and stuffed rolls of meat such as beef olives. In fact, the slow cooker is ideal for dumplings as the temperature is low enough for a gentle simmer so they won't break up. Models differ but generally you should switch the cooker to the high setting about a quarter of an hour before cooking the dumplings and after the main cooking period of the meat dish. Form the dough into small balls and put on top of the meat. Cover and leave for ½–1½ hours depending on your manufacturer's instructions. For small slow cookers, make a smaller quantity of dough and roll into a 'sausage roll' to fit the pan. Then cook for just half an hour . . . and remember, no peeking! Otherwise you will let all the steam out.

Stuffed rolls of meat can be cooked on the low setting (after an initial high setting for half an hour) for 5–6 hours. Puddings, in 0.55 litre to 1.1 litre/1 to 2 pint basins only, can be boiled on the high setting for about 3–6 hours, depending on how rich the mixture is, whilst a Christmas pudding will take a total of 20 hours or more – but then you don't have to keep topping up the water level and there will be no steam escaping all over the kitchen, so this could be an ideal way of cooking it. *Models differ so do check your instruction book first* to check when you should switch from high to low or vice versa.

FREEZING SUET DISHES

These freeze better uncooked. Prepare in the usual way up to the cooking stage, then pack in special heatproof and freezer proof glass containers or foil. Seal with pleated greaseproof and foil as normal and label – most important if you want to ensure you eat the right dish at the right course!

To cook, there is no need to thaw. Follow the instructions on page 15 for boiling and steaming and add about 20 minutes to the time. To cook from frozen in a pressure cooker, add a cupful more boiling water than normal and an extra 10 minutes onto the steaming time before bringing to pressure. To cook in a microwave oven from frozen, add a couple of extra minutes onto the total cooking time, which means effectively giving the pudding another 'burst' of power (see page 18). Refer first though to your manufacturer's instruction book, as ovens do differ.

Main Meals

Steak and Kidney Pudding and Pie
Serves 4–6   (pictures on pages 23 and 27)

A rich and tasty homemade steak and kidney pudding or
pie is always a well received dish. I often serve a special
pie made with a rough red wine and a suet shortcut or
flaky pastry for a winter's evening dinner party or, using
the same filling, as a pudding for a Sunday lunch, sent to
the table in the old fashioned manner, still in the
basin and wrapped in a white damask napkin.

Pastry
Either flaky pastry made with 250 g/8 oz flour (see page 9).
Or   shortcut pastry made with 250 g/8 oz flour and eggs for
        a quick pie.
Or   for a pudding, 250 g/8 oz flour (see page 7).
Filling

750 g	lean braising steak	1½ lbs
250 g	lamb's *or* ox kidney	8 oz
2 × 15 ml spoons	flour	2 tablespoons
3 × 15 ml spoons	vegetable oil	3 tablespoons
1	large onion, sliced	1
250 ml	rough red wine *or* beer	½ pint
250 ml	good beef stock	½ pint
	a bouquet garni	

Method
1 Cut the meat into even-sized pieces and coat in the
flour.
2 Heat the oil and fry the onion until soft and transparent, about 10 minutes. Remove to a plate.
3 Brown the meat in the oil, adding a little extra if
required. Return the fried onion and pour in the wine or
beer and stock.
4 Bring to the boil, stirring and scraping up the sedi-
ment on the pan base, it all adds to the flavour. Add the
herbs.

5 Place in an ovenproof casserole, cover and cook at 180°C/350°F/Gas Mark 4 for 2–2½ hours until just tender. Do not overcook as there will be extra cooking time with the pastry.

6 Drain any excess gravy and reserve to use as a gravy when serving. Allow to cool, if possible overnight. Use as desired for a pudding or pie in a 1.1 litre/2 pint basin or pie dish following the guidelines on pages 13 and 14.

Boiled Beef with Oaty Mustard Dumplings
Serves 4–6   (picture on page 27)

Like so many of our traditional dishes, boiled beef is not served often enough. The term 'boiled' is probably partly to blame, although in fact, salted or unsalted beef is gently poached with light dumplings in a flavoursome stock, a little of which is then served as a gravy.

1.5 kg	piece of brisket *or* topside *or* silverside, preferably salted	3 lb
1	onion, quartered	1
3–4	carrots	3–4
2–3	celery sticks	2–3
1	turnip, peeled and quartered	1
1.25 ml spoon	black peppercorns	¼ teaspoon
1	bouquet garni	1
2	bay leaves	2
Dumplings		
100 g	self-raising flour	4 oz
25 g	porridge oats	1 oz
50 g	shredded suet	2 oz
2 × 5 ml spoons	French mustard	2 teaspoons
	water, to mix	
	pinch of salt	

Method

1 If the beef is salted then soak overnight in cold water and drain. Place in a large heavy saucepan and cover with cold water.

2 Bring slowly to the boil and skim off any scum that rises to the top. Drop in the vegetables, peppercorns and herbs. If you are cooking an unsalted piece then add salt to taste. Cover and simmer gently allowing 25 minutes per 500 g/lb and 25 minutes over or until tender.

3 Remove the beef to a warm plate and using a slotted draining spoon, try to scoop out the vegetables and as many peppercorns as possible, discarding the peppercorns.

4 Make up the dumplings by mixing the flour, oats, salt and suet together. Mix the mustard with a tablespoon of water and add this together with extra water to the flour, mixing till you have a firm, soft dough. Form into small balls, allowing two to three per person. Drop these into the simmering stock, cover and cook very gently for 15–20 minutes or until risen and cooked.

5 Serve the beef sliced, surrounded by the vegetables and dumplings. Strain the stock and use some as an unthickened gravy. Sprinkle the meat platter with a little chopped parsley, if liked.

Chilli Beef Roll (picture on page 35)
Serves 4

Filling		
1	medium onion, chopped	1
1	clove of garlic, crushed	1
2 × 15 ml spoons	vegetable oil	2 tablespoons
250 g	minced beef	8 oz
1	red pimento (pepper), canned, *or* fresh, chopped	1
2 × 5 ml spoons	mild chilli powder salt and ground black pepper	2 teaspoons
Pastry		
150 g	self-raising flour, sifted	6 oz
75 g	shredded suet water, to mix	3 oz

Veal and ham raised pie (p. 45), Traditional steak and kidney pie (p. 20), Lamb Wellington (p. 28)

Method
1 Fry the onion and garlic in the oil until softened. Add the mince and brown, then add the pimento and chilli powder. Season, cover and cook very gently for about 20 minutes.
2 Make the pastry (see page 7) and roll out to a large rectangle, 5 mm/¼ in. thick.
3 Spread the mince mixture on it, roll up and trim the edges.
4 Place on a baking sheet, glaze with a little milk if liked, and bake at 190°C/375°F/Gas Mark 5 for about 30 minutes. Serve with a quick tomato sauce.

Quick Tomato Sauce
Fry a small chopped onion in a little vegetable oil with two rashers of smoked bacon, chopped. When softened, about 5 minutes, add a 425 g/15 oz can of peeled tomatoes, a 15 ml spoon/1 tablespoon of tomato purée, a 15 ml spoon/1 tablespoon Worcestershire sauce, pinch of sugar, salt and ground black pepper and a good pinch of marjoram, oregano or basil. Cover and simmer for 15 minutes, then either blend in a liquidiser for a smooth sauce, or mush slightly with a fork.

Rolled Belly of Pork with Apple and Ginger Stuffing
Serves 6   (picture on page 31)

A lean belly of pork can make a tasty and inexpensive roast suitable even for a Sunday lunch. You'll need a large whole piece of pork and if you don't feel capable of boning it yourself, then ask your butcher to do so for you. Leave some rind on the side you intend to be the top when you've rolled it for crisp crackling, but remove the rest so that it is not rolled inside with the stuffing. Score the remaining rind with a very sharp knife or even a handyman's razor knife. With apple in this stuffing, there is no need to serve apple sauce, but try adding some dry cider to the gravy when you make it with the pan juices.

1.5 kg	lean belly of pork in one piece, boned	3 lb
Stuffing		
75 g	fresh white breadcrumbs	3 oz
40 g	shredded suet	1½ oz
1	small onion, finely chopped	1
1	large cooking apple, peeled and grated	1
2 × 5 ml spoons	ground ginger	2 teaspoons
5 ml spoon	dried rubbed sage	1 teaspoon
1	size 3 egg, beaten	1
1	lemon, rind only	1
	salt and ground black pepper	

Method

1 First prepare the pork as necessary and lightly season the boned side to be rolled up.

2 Mix the stuffing ingredients together and spread over the seasoned meat. Roll up firmly, but not too tightly and tie at about 5 cm/2 in. intervals. If possible, try to keep some rind for the top of the joint if you want crackling, and make sure it is well scored. Rub with some salt and do not baste during cooking.

3 Roast at 180°C/350°F/Gas Mark 4 allowing 30 minutes per 500 g/1 lb plus 30 minutes over, that is about 2 hours. Allow to stand for 15 minutes before carving to let the meat and stuffing 'set', so that it is easier to carve.

NB If liked, make up extra stuffing, shape it into long rolls and roast with the meat. Serve with the joint and vegetables such as courgettes and carrots.

Beef Olives
Serves 4–6

Although by no means difficult to make, beef olives do take a little time because of the number of preparation stages – but they are certainly worth it. Serve on a china plate, surrounded by a border of piped potato, if possible.

6 thin slices of lean beef, e.g. topside, rump or buttock, approx. 7.5 × 6.5 cm/3 × 2½ in.

Stuffing

100 g	fresh white breadcrumbs	4 oz
50 g	shredded suet	2 oz
2 × 15 ml spoons	chopped fresh parsley	2 tablespoons
2 × 5 ml spoons	lemon rind, grated	2 teaspoons
	salt and ground black pepper	
1	egg, size 3 or 4, beaten	1

Mirepoix and sauce

1	carrot, peeled and chopped	1
1	onion, peeled and chopped	1
1	small turnip, peeled and chopped	1
1	celery stick, chopped	1
1	leek, chopped	1
50 g	butter	2 oz
375 ml	beef stock	¾ pint
	cornflour, to thicken, optional	
2 × 15 ml spoons	dry sherry, optional	2 tablespoons

Method

1 Beat the slices of beef between sheets of wet grease-proof paper and trim to a neat shape.

2 Mix together the stuffing ingredients, using the egg to bind and spread a little on each of the meat slices.

3 Roll up and tie with fine cotton string, or skewer with wooden cocktail sticks.

4 Fry the vegetables in the butter for a few minutes and place on the base of a deep casserole. Season well.

5 Fry the meat rolls in the remaining butter to seal, and arrange on top of the vegetables.

6 Pour over the stock, cover and cook for 2 hours at 160°C/325°F/Gas Mark 3.

7 Strain off the liquor and thicken with a little cornflour, or blend in a liquidiser. Add the sherry if liked and re-heat gently. Serve hot with a border of piped, creamed potato and coat the beef olives with the sauce.

Boiled beef (p. 21), Traditional steak and kidney pudding (p. 20), Beef olives

Lamb Wellington (picture on page 23)
Serves 3–4

Buy a best end of neck with the whole length of the cutlet on it – not a shortened one – for this dish.

Flaky pastry		
250 g	plain flour	8 oz
2.5 ml spoon	salt	½ teaspoon
15 ml spoon	lemon juice	1 tablespoon
90 g	shredded suet	3 oz
90 g	butter, creamed	3 oz
	iced water, to mix	

1 Best end of lamb, with about 7 cutlets on it, *chined only*		
1–2	cloves garlic, crushed	1–2
5 ml spoon	rosemary	1 teaspoon
	salt and ground black pepper	
100 g	smooth mild pâté	4 oz
1	egg, size 3, beaten	1

Method

1 First, make up the flaky pastry (see page 9) then allow to rest in the fridge whilst you prepare the meat.
2 With a sharp boning or thin knife, cut away the bones of the lamb, leaving a long 'fillet' part down one side and a large 'flap' to roll over it. Alternatively, ask your butcher to do this for you.
3 Season with garlic, rosemary and seasoning. Roll up fairly tightly and tie in about four places with fine cotton string, or secure with skewers, although you do not get such a tight roll with skewers. Roast at 180°C/350°F/Gas Mark 4 for 45 minutes, if you like your lamb slightly pink inside, or 1 hour if you prefer it well done.
4 Allow to cool, then smear all over with pâté.
5 Roll out the pastry to 5 mm/¼ in. thick, so that it is large enough to completely cover the joint. Cut out four 5 cm/2 in. squares at the corners, so that the pastry will not be as thick at the ends when you come to fold it.
6 Place the pâté covered joint in the centre of the pastry and fold firmly over to enclose, damping and pinching the edges to seal.

7 Place the roll, join side down on a greased baking sheet. Cut pastry leaves or other decorations from the trimmings and fix these to the top with beaten egg. Glaze well all over and bake at 200°C/400°F/Gas Mark 6 for 30 minutes, or until golden and crisp.

Mrs Leech's Lamb Hot Pot with Crunchy Dumplings
Serves 4

This recipe brings back fond memories of student days when my landlady served a delicious hot pot with wonderful dumplings. Whether the dumplings were meant to be crunchy on top, or had gone so because we were always late home, I don't know – but they were good!

500–750 g	boned stewing lamb, lean breast *or* shoulder	1–1½ lbs
3 × 15 ml spoons	vegetable oil	3 tablespoons
1	onion, sliced	1
2	carrots, peeled and sliced	2
2 × 15 ml spoons	flour	2 tablespoons
375 ml	stock	¾ pint
2	bay leaves	2
	salt and ground black pepper	
225 g can	butter beans, drained	8 oz can
Dumplings		
150 g	self-raising flour	6 oz
75 g	shredded suet	3 oz
1	lemon, rind only	1
5 ml spoon	mixed dried herbs	1 teaspoon
	salt and ground black pepper	
	water, to mix	

Method

1 Cut the meat into cubes and fry quickly in the oil to brown. Remove to a plate. Add the onion and carrots to the pan and fry gently until softened, about 10 minutes.
2 Stir in the flour, then add the stock and bring to the boil, stirring until thickened. Add the bay leaves and seasoning and return the meat. Transfer to an oven-

proof casserole dish, cover and cook for 1 hour at 180°C/
350°F/Gas Mark 4.

3 Stir in the butter beans. Make up the dumplings and
divide into eight balls. Drop into the hot pot, cover
again and return to the oven for about another 30
minutes, uncovering after 15 minutes to let the
dumplings go crunchy and browned on top. Serve hot
with green leafy vegetables or leeks.

Stuffed Lamb's Hearts with Sherry Sauce
Serves 4

4	lamb's hearts	4
2 × 15 ml spoons	vegetable oil	2 tablespoons
Stuffing		
50 g	fresh white breadcrumbs	2 oz
25 g	shredded suet	1 oz
15 ml spoon	fresh chopped parsley	1 tablespoon
5 ml spoon	dried savory *or* thyme	1 teaspoon
5 ml spoon	grated lemon rind	1 teaspoon
1	egg, size 3, beaten	1
1.25 ml spoon	ground mace *or* nutmeg	¼ teaspoon
	salt and ground black pepper	
Mirepoix and stock		
1	onion, chopped	1
1	carrot, chopped	1
1	celery stick, chopped	1
250 ml	stock	½ pint
1	bay leaf	1
	salt and ground black pepper	
15 ml spoon	cornflour	1 tablespoon
2 × 15 ml spoons	sherry, dry *or* medium	2 tablespoons

Method

1 Prepare the hearts by trimming away the fat and
cutting out the gristle and any tubes. Cut through the
central muscle to make one larger cavity. Soak in salted
cold water for 30 minutes, then rinse and pat dry.

Stuffed lamb's hearts, Mrs Leech's lamb hot pot (p. 29),
Rolled belly of pork (p. 24)

2 Mix all the stuffing ingredients together and stuff well into each heart.

3 Using a darning needle or trussing needle and strong cotton thread, stitch the top of the hearts, and any other cuts made by the butcher, together to enclose stuffing.

4 Heat the oil in a frying pan, or a cast-iron casserole, and brown the hearts. Remove and fry the mirepoix vegetables in the oil until softened, about 5 minutes, then place on the base of an ovenproof casserole. Stand the hearts on the vegetables and pour in the stock. Add the bay leaf and seasonings.

5 Cover and cook at 160°C/325°F/Gas Mark 3 for 2½ hours or until tender.

6 Remove the bay leaf. If you like a smooth sauce and if you have a blender, blend the vegetables and stock, or rub through a sieve with a wooden spoon. Otherwise leave the sauce 'chunky'.

7 Blend the cornflour with a little cold water and stir into the puréed vegetable stock. Bring to the boil, stirring continually until smooth and thick, allow to simmer for a minute, then stir in the sherry. Taste the sauce for seasoning, adjust if necessary and pour over the hearts. Serve hot, garnished with chopped parsley, if liked.

Chicken and Ham Loaf (picture on page 39)
Serves 4

4–6	rashers streaky bacon, de-rinded	4–6
1	small onion, peeled and chopped	1
100 g	mushrooms, chopped	4 oz
15 g	butter	½ oz
75 g	shredded suet	3 oz
100 g	cooked chicken, chopped	4 oz
100 g	cooked ham, chopped	4 oz
150 g	fresh white breadcrumbs	6 oz
2 × 15 ml spoons	chopped parsley	2 tablespoons
	salt and ground black pepper	
1	egg, size 3, beaten	1

Method
1 Cut the bacon rashers in half and stretch with the back of a knife.
2 Grease a 1 kg/2 lb loaf tin and line the base and sides with the bacon, and, if preferred, a sheet of greased greaseproof paper.
3 Gently fry the onion and mushrooms in the butter until soft, about 10 minutes, then mix thoroughly with the remaining ingredients.
4 Transfer the mixture into the loaf tin and bake at 200°C/400°F/Gas Mark 6 for 40 minutes, or until cooked.
5 Turn out to serve.

Pork Terrine en Crôute (picture on front cover)
Serves 6

Terrine		
250 g	belly of pork, minced	8 oz
100 g	streaky bacon, chopped	4 oz
100 g	pig's liver, chopped	4 oz
1	medium onion, chopped	1
1–2	garlic cloves, crushed	1–2
2 × 15 ml spoons	dry sherry *or* brandy	2 tablespoons
2 × 15 ml spoons	fresh chopped parsley	2 tablespoons
2.5 ml spoon	dried thyme	½ teaspoon
scant 5 ml spoon	salt	¾ teaspoon
	ground black pepper	
Pastry		
250 g	self-raising flour, sifted	8 oz
125 g	shredded suet	4 oz
	pinch of salt	
1	egg, size 3, beaten	1
	beaten egg, to glaze	

Method
1 Pre-heat oven to 180°C/350°F/Gas Mark 4 and lightly grease a 1 kg/2 lb loaf tin, preferably with drop-down sides.
2 Prepare and mix all the terrine ingredients together.
3 Mix the flour, suet and salt together, then bind with the beaten egg, adding cold water if necessary to make a stiff dough.

4 Roll out three-quarters of the pastry on a lightly floured surface into a large oblong about 5 mm/¼ in. thick and use to line the loaf tin.

5 Fill with the terrine mixture. Roll out the remaining pastry and put on the top. Seal the edges with a little beaten egg, trim, crimp and glaze.

6 Make pastry leaves or decorations with any trimmings (see page 13). Glaze these too.

7 Bake for 55–60 minutes until golden brown and cooked, covering half way through, if over browning, with foil.

8 Allow to cool completely before turning out.

NB If you do not have a tin with drop-down sides, place a long strip of treble thickness foil down the sides of the tin with enough overhang to pull the terrine out when cooked.

Wheaty Liver Loaf
Serves 4–6

250 g	chicken *or* lamb's livers, chopped	8 oz
100 g	streaky bacon, chopped	4 oz
1	small onion, chopped	1
1	garlic clove, crushed, optional	1
2 × 15 ml spoons	vegetable oil	2 tablespoons
15 ml spoon	flour	1 tablespoon
250 ml	stock	½ pint
5 ml spoon	marjoram	1 teaspoon
15 ml spoon	tomato pureé	1 tablespoon
	salt and ground black pepper	
Pastry dough		
100 g	self-raising flour	4 oz
100 g	wholemeal flour	4 oz
100 g	shredded suet	4 oz
2 × 5 ml spoons	baking powder	2 teaspoons
2 × 15 ml spoons	chopped fresh parsley	2 tablespoons
	water, to mix	

Chilli beef roll (p. 22), Wheaty liver loaf, Leek and bacon pie (p. 42)

Method

1 Fry the liver, bacon, onion and garlic (if used) in the oil until brown and softened, about 5 minutes.

2 Stir in the flour, then gradually add the stock, stirring continuously. Bring to the boil, add the marjoram and tomato purée, season to taste and simmer for about 10 minutes, uncovered, so that the liquid becomes reduced. Allow to cool whilst you make the dough.

3 Grease a 1 kg/2 lb loaf tin and line the base with greased greaseproof paper.

4 Mix the flours, suet, baking powder and parsley together, then add enough water to mix to a firm dough.

5 Divide the dough into four and roll out in rectangles to fit the loaf tin, you may have to make the base slightly smaller than the top.

6 Place a layer of dough on the greaseproof paper, trimming to fit if necessary or moulding gently with your fingers. Top with a third of the liver mixture. Continue with dough and liver layers, finishing with dough.

7 Cover with greased greaseproof paper and foil and bake at 180°C/350°F/Gas Mark 4 for about 1 hour. Turn out onto a warm serving plate and serve hot with a good rich gravy or tomato sauce (see page 24).

Greek Stuffed Vegetables

Vegetables such as aubergines, peppers, courgettes and tomatoes (especially the large Mediterranean types) make substantial, tasty and inexpensive meals when scooped out and filled with delicious stuffings. Shredded suet is ideal for these stuffings as it gives a firmer texture and richer flavour. Instead of sticking to one vegetable, choose a variety for an attractive presentation, topped with dollops of natural yogurt, if liked, and served with just a crisp green salad and crusty or pitta bread.

Allow two vegetables per head and try to buy ones of roughly the same size, e.g. large tomatoes, small aubergines, medium peppers, etc.

For four whole vegetables allow

The scooped out and prepared flesh (see below)

100 g	long grain rice, boiled	4 oz
1	clove garlic, crushed	1
1	small onion, chopped	1
15 ml spoon	vegetable oil	1 tablespoon
5 ml spoon	ground cumin	1 teaspoon
50 g	shredded suet	2 oz
100 g	cooked ham, beef, lamb *or* chicken, chopped	4 oz
1	egg, size 3, beaten salt and ground black pepper	1
125 g carton	natural unsweetened yogurt, optional	5 oz carton

To prepare the vegetables

Aubergines and courgettes Cut in half lengthways and slash the flesh with a sharp knife. Sprinkle with cooking salt and leave to stand for 30 minutes. Drain and rinse off the bitter juices and salt, then scoop out most of the flesh and chop finely. Blanch the shells in boiling water for about 5 minutes until softened slightly and drain well. Add the chopped flesh at stage 1 in the method.

Green peppers Cut off the tops and discard the stalks. Scoop out the hot seeds inside and discard. Blanch the shells and tops in boiling water until slightly softened, about 5 minutes.

Tomatoes Cut off the tops and reserve, then scoop out the seeds and some flesh. Chop and add both to the stuffing at stage 1.

Onions Peel, leave whole and boil for about 15 minutes until softened. Remove the centre with a teaspoon and chop the flesh. Add to the stuffing at stage 1.

Method

1 Fry the garlic, onion and chosen chopped vegetable flesh in the oil until soft, about 10 minutes. Add the cumin and cook for another minute.

2 Stir in the rice, meat, egg, suet and seasoning.

3 Spoon into the vegetable shells, piling high in the centre. Cover the peppers and tomatoes with their tops.

Cover and bake at 180°C/350°F/Gas Mark 4 for 1 hour, uncovering for the last 15 minutes to brown.

4 Serve hot, attractively arranged on a platter with dollops of yogurt on top, if liked.

Old English Chicken Pie (picture on page 43)
Serves 4–6

An old fashioned way of stretching a small amount of leftover chicken to feed the family, which is still highly appropriate for today.

Forcemeat balls		
100 g	fresh white breadcrumbs	4 oz
50 g	shredded suet	2 oz
5 ml spoon	fresh chopped parsley	1 teaspoon
2.5 ml spoon	dried mixed herbs	½ teaspoon
5 ml spoon	lemon juice	1 teaspoon
1	egg, size 3, beaten	1
Filling		
25 g	butter	1 oz
4	chipolata sausages, chopped	4
15 ml spoon	flour	1 tablespoon
250 ml	chicken stock	½ pint
	salt and ground black pepper	
150 g	cooked chicken, diced	6 oz
Pastry		
Either	flaky pastry made with 100 g/4 oz flour (see page 9).	
Or	shortcut pastry made with 100 g/4 oz flour and an egg (see page 7).	

Method
1 Mix all the forcemeat ingredients together and form into eight small balls.
2 Melt the butter and fry the forcemeat balls and sausages until golden. Place in a deep pie dish.
3 Stir the flour into the remaining butter and cook for a minute, then gradually stir in the stock, stirring continuously until thickened.

Chicken and ham loaf (p. 32), Greek stuffed vegetables (p. 36)

4 Bring to the boil, season and add the chicken. Pour over the forcemeat balls and sausages.

5 Roll out the chosen pastry to fit the pie dish, about 5 mm/¼ in. thick. Cover the filling (see page 13), decorate as desired with trimmings, glaze with a little beaten egg or milk and bake at 220°C/425°F/Gas Mark 7 for 20–25 minutes until golden brown and crisp. Serve hot.

Chicken Stew Soup with Basil Dumplings
Serves 4

1	chicken carcass	1
2	onions, 1 chopped, 1 quartered	2
4	celery sticks, chopped	4
1 litre	water	2 pints
2	bay leaves	2
	salt and ground black pepper	
25 g	butter *or* margarine	1 oz
15 ml spoon	flour	1 tablespoon
425 g can	tomatoes	15 oz can
5 ml spoon (*or* 2.5 ml spoon)	fresh chopped basil (*or* dried rubbed basil)	1 teaspoon (*or* ½ teaspoon)
5 ml spoon	sugar	1 teaspoon
15 ml spoon	Worcestershire sauce	1 tablespoon
375–400 g	cold cooked chicken cut into chunks	10–12 oz
Dumplings		
100 g	self-raising flour, sifted	4 oz
50 g	shredded suet	2 oz
5 ml spoon (*or* 2.5 ml spoon)	fresh chopped basil (*or* dried rubbed basil)	1 teaspoon (*or* ½ teaspoon)
	salt and ground black pepper	
	water, to mix	

Method

1 Make a good stock by boiling the carcass with 1 quartered onion, 1 stick of celery, 1 litre/2 pints of water, bay leaves, salt and pepper for a good 30 minutes, then strain and reserve.

2 Melt the butter or margarine and sweat the remaining onions and celery for 10 minutes, that is cover and fry very gently indeed. The vegetables should be soft and not at all browned.

3 Stir in the flour and cook for a minute. Strain in the juice of the canned tomatoes, then roughly chop the tomatoes, and add these to the pot together with the reserved stock. Bring to the boil, stirring.

4 Add the basil, sugar, Worcestershire sauce and seasoning. Simmer for 15 minutes, then stir in the chicken pieces.

5 Make the dumplings (see page 8) and divide into eight balls. Drop into the pot and simmer very gently for 20 minutes until the dumplings are risen and cooked.

6 Serve hot in large soup bowls sprinkled with a little fresh or dried basil, if liked.

Tarragon Turkey Rolls with Orange Walnut Stuffing
Serves 3

3 × 100 g	turkey breast fillets	3 × 4 oz
Stuffing		
100 g	fresh white breadcrumbs	4 oz
50 g	shredded suet	2 oz
1	small onion, chopped finely	1
5 ml spoon (*or* 2 × 5 ml spoons)	dried tarragon (*or* chopped fresh)	1 teaspoon (*or* 2 teaspoons)
25 g	chopped walnuts	1 oz
1	orange, rind and juice	1
1	egg, size 3	1
	salt and ground black pepper	
Sauce		
250 ml	chicken stock	½ pint
20 g	butter	¾ oz
20 g	flour	¾ oz
2 × 15 ml spoons	dry sherry	2 tablespoons
2 × 15 ml spoons	cream	2 tablespoons

Method

1 Trim the turkey breast into neat oblongs, then place

between two sheets of wet greaseproof paper. Beat well with a rolling pin until quite thin.

2 Mix the stuffing ingredients together and reserve half the orange juice for the sauce.

3 Spread the stuffing on the meat then roll up tightly and place join side down on a greased baking dish. Season lightly, pour over the stock and add a couple of bay leaves, if liked.

4 Cover and bake for about 25 minutes at 200°C/400°F/Gas Mark 6 or until cooked. Remove the rolls to a serving dish and keep warm. Reserve the stock.

5 For the sauce, melt the butter, add the flour and stir to a roux, or thick paste. Cook for a minute, then strain in the turkey stock gradually, stirring continually until smooth and thickened. Add the reserved orange juice and sherry and allow to simmer for two minutes.

6 Remove from the heat and stir in the cream. Check the seasoning and carefully spoon over the turkey rolls.

7 Serve hot, garnished with orange slices and sprinkled with a little dried tarragon, or some small fresh sprigs if available.

Leek and Bacon Pie (picture on page 35)
Serves 4–6

100 g	self-raising flour, sifted	4 oz
100 g	wholemeal flour, sifted	4 oz
100 g	shredded suet	4 oz
5 ml spoon	baking powder	1 teaspoon
	pinch of salt	
1	egg, size 3, beaten	1
	water, to mix	
Filling		
250 g	bacon, chopped	8 oz
25 g	butter	1 oz
500 g	leeks, washed and sliced	1 lb
100 g	mushrooms, sliced	4 oz
2	eggs, size 3, beaten	2
2.5 ml spoon	dried thyme	½ teaspoon
	salt and ground black pepper	

Chicken stew soup (p. 40), Old English chicken pie (p. 38), Tarragon turkey rolls (p. 41)

Method

1 Mix the flours, suet, baking powder and salt to a firm dough with the egg and water. Divide the pastry in two and roll out both pieces to fit the top and base of a 20 cm/ 8 in. pie dish. Line the base with pastry.

2 Meanwhile, fry the bacon gently in the butter, then add the prepared leeks. Cover the pan and cook very gently for 10 minutes, then add the mushrooms and cook for a few minutes more.

3 Remove from the heat and stir in the eggs, thyme and seasoning.

4 Spoon into the pastry base. Damp the edges, top with the remaining pastry, seal and crimp the edges (see page 13). Make a cross or slits in the top of the pastry, glaze with milk or a little more beaten egg and decorate with pastry trimmings, if liked.

5 Stand on a baking sheet and bake at 190°C/375°F/Gas Mark 5 for 30 minutes or until browned and crisp.

A Grand Fish Pie
Serves 4

Home-made fish pies are fast coming back into favour and many tasty recipes are available which can either stretch more expensive species such as cod to feed more, or make newer, cheaper species like coley more acceptable to cautious family palates.

Either	Suet flaky pastry using 250 g/8 oz quantity of flour (see page 9).	
Or	Shortcut pastry using 150 g/6 oz flour and an egg (see page 7).	
500 g	white fish fillets *or* steaks e.g. haddock, cod, coley, whiting	1 lb
150 ml	dry cider	¼ pint
150 ml	water	¼ pint
1	bay leaf	1
1 (*or* 1.25 ml spoon)	blade of mace (*or* nutmeg)	1 (*or* ¼ teaspoon)
	salt and ground black pepper	

Sauce

25 g	butter	1 oz
1	onion, chopped	1
25 g	flour	1 oz
150 ml	milk	¼ pint
2 × 15 ml spoons	single cream, optional	2 tablespoons
50 g	mushrooms, quartered	2 oz
50 g	frozen prawns, optional	2 oz
2	tomatoes, skinned, quartered and de-seeded	2
15 ml spoon	fresh chopped parsley	1 tablespoon
	beaten egg *or* milk to glaze	

Method

1 First, make the pastry if using the flaky recipe.

2 Poach the fish in the cider and water with the bay leaf, mace and seasoning at 190°C/375°F/Gas Mark 5 for 20 minutes, or until cooked. Strain and reserve the liquor. Skin and flake the fish.

3 Melt the butter and gently fry the onion for 10 minutes until soft. Stir in the flour and cook for a minute, then gradually stir in the reserved fish liquor and milk. Bring to the boil, still stirring until smooth and thickened. Simmer for 2 minutes, then remove from the heat and stir in the cream, if used. Season well.

4 Stir in the mushrooms, prawns (if used), tomatoes, parsley and flaked fish.

5 Pour into a 1.1 litre/2 pint pie dish.

6 If using shortcut pastry, make this now. Roll out the pastry and cover the dish (see page 13). Decorate as desired with the trimmings, cut a cross in the centre of the pastry, glaze with milk or beaten egg and bake at 200°C/400°F/Gas Mark 6 for 30 minutes or until golden.

Veal and Ham Raised Pie (picture on page 23)
Serves 4–6

Prepare the filling first for this pie, as the pastry should be moulded and cooked as soon after making as possible. Omit the eggs if a round tin is to be used – it's difficult to share them out!

Filling

500–750 g	pie veal, diced	1–1½ lb
250 g	lean bacon in one piece (*or* bacon chops), diced	8 oz
1	onion, chopped	1
1	lemon, rind only	1
2.5 ml spoon	dried rubbed sage	½ teaspoon
	salt and ground black pepper	
2	eggs, hard boiled, optional	2
2 × 5 ml spoons	gelatine	2 teaspoons
250 ml	stock	½ pint

Pastry

100 g	shredded suet	4 oz
125 ml	water and milk, mixed	¼ pint
300 g	self-raising flour, sifted	12 oz
5 ml spoon	salt	1 teaspoon
	beaten egg to glaze	

Method

1 First prepare the tin. Use a 18 cm/7 in. round, or a 1 kg/2 lb loaf tin or a medium-size special raised pie mould. In all cases try to choose a tin with a loose base or spring sides, otherwise you should mould a treble thick band of foil about 7.5 cm/3 in. wide inside the tin allowing sufficient overhang on the outside to lift out the cooked pie. Grease the tin well, whatever the shape, including the foil band if used.

2 Mix all the filling ingredients together except for the eggs, gelatine and stock.

3 In a medium-size pan, slowly heat the suet and milky water until melted. When *all* the fat has melted, bring to a brisk boil and immediately tip in all the flour plus salt. Beat hard with a wooden spoon until the mixture thickens up and leaves the sides of the bowl as one mass.

4 Remove from the heat and cut off a quarter for the top of the pie. Put the rest of the pastry into the tin and using your fingers and knuckles push and mould the pastry along the base and up the sides. If it helps, you can roll it out a bit on a lightly floured surface first and

Haddock gougère (p. 48), A grand fish pie (p. 44)

then mould to fit. Make sure the base and sides do not have any tears or are too thin, and that there is sufficient pastry at the top to seal to the top pastry cover.

5 Fill with the filling, placing hard boiled eggs in the centre if using a loaf or mould tin. Roll out the remaining pastry for the top and fit over the filling, damping and sealing the edges first with a little beaten egg. Trim excess pastry and cut a hole in the centre.

6 Depending on your artistic flair, decorate with the trimmings (see page 13), glaze well with the beaten egg and bake at 200°C/400°F/Gas Mark 6 for 20 minutes, then lower the heat to 180°C/350°F/Gas Mark 4 for a further 2 hours. Cover with foil, if the top is browning too quickly.

7 Whilst the pie is cooling, make up the jelly stock. Sprinkle the gelatine onto two tablespoons (2 × 15 ml spoons) of cold water. Allow to swell and turn solid, then slowly heat until dissolved. Do not boil. Add the stock and slowly pour into the pie through the centre hole. Allow to get quite cold before turning out, although a raised pie is very nice to eat hot without the jelly stock.

Haddock Gougère (picture on page 47)
Serves 4–6

A gougère is a savoury choux pastry ring filled with a creamy meat or fish sauce.

Pastry ring		
75 g	plain flour	3 oz
	pinch of salt	
75 g	shredded suet	3 oz
200 ml	water	7½ fl oz
3	eggs, size 3, beaten	3
50 g	Cheddar cheese, grated	2 oz
Filling		
250 g	smoked haddock fillet	8 oz
250 ml	milk	½ pint
1	bay leaf	1
40 g	butter	1½ oz
50 g	mushrooms, sliced	2 oz

I	small onion, chopped	I
10 ml spoon	mild curry powder	I dessertspoon
25 g	flour	I oz
15 ml spoon	lemon juice	I tablespoon
	salt and ground black pepper	

Method

1 Sift the flour and salt together. Slowly melt the suet in the water, then when all the suet has melted, bring it to the boil.

2 Tip all the flour in at once and beat hard until the mixture forms a ball and leaves the side of the pan. Allow to cool for about 10 minutes.

3 Gradually beat in the eggs until the mixture drops fairly easily when jerked from the spoon. You may not need all the eggs, and the mixture should not be too soft. Stir in the cheese.

4 On a greased and wet baking sheet (the water gives off steam to help the initial rise) form an oblong with the pastry, or pipe into one using a plain nozzle. Bake at 200°C/400°F/Gas Mark 6 for about 20–25 minutes until well risen and golden. Remove from the oven and with a sharp knife slit round the outside to allow the steam to escape, then return to the oven for a further 5 minutes to allow the inside to dry out.

5 Meanwhile, poach the haddock in the same oven with the milk, bay leaf, 15 g/½ oz of the butter, and the seasoning, for about 20 minutes or until cooked. Remove the fish (reserving the liquor), skin and flake.

6 Melt the remaining butter and fry the mushrooms and onions until soft, about 10 minutes. Stir in the curry powder and cook for a further minute, then add the flour and cook for yet another minute.

7 Strain and gradually stir in the fish liquor until smooth. Bring to the boil, add the lemon juice and seasoning and simmer for 2 minutes, then add the flaked fish and re-heat.

8 Spoon the filling into the hollow of the ring. Serve hot with the centre of the ring garnished with watercress.

Sweet Puddings and Desserts

Old English Treacle Tart
Serves 4–6

Pastry		
150 g	self-raising flour, sifted	6 oz
75 g	shredded suet	3 oz
	pinch of salt	
1	egg, size 3, beaten	1
	milk, to mix	
Filling		
25 g (*or* 25 g) (*or* 50 g)	porridge oat flakes (*or* desiccated coconut) (*or* fresh white breadcrumbs)	1 oz (*or* 1 oz) (*or* 2 oz)
8 × 15 ml spoons	golden syrup	8 tablespoons
1	lemon, rind and juice, a little egg white and caster sugar, to glaze	1

Method

1 Make the pastry (see page 7) and roll out to 5 mm/ ¼ in. thick. Line a 20 cm/8 in. flan dish or ring set on a baking sheet. Prick the base and bake blind (see page 12).

2 Sprinkle the base with the oat flakes, coconut or breadcrumbs and add the syrup. To spoon it in easily, either stand the tin in a pan of simmering water and spoon out when melted, or heat a tablespoon over a gas flame or in boiling water and use it to spoon out the syrup, which will fall off easily. Sprinkle over the rind and lemon juice.

3 Using the trimmings, roll out to 25 cm/10 in. thin strips and make a lattice on the top, twisting it if you have the time and patience.

Strawberry cream cake (p. 65), Two fruits meringue pie (p. 52), Old English treacle tart, Rhubarb and mallow flan (p. 64)

4 Brush the strips with egg white and sprinkle with sugar for a nice sparkle when baked.

5 Bake at 190°C/375°F/Gas Mark 5 for 20 minutes until golden and baked. Serve warm (not hot, otherwise it will burn) or cold with cream, custard or the soured cream sauce on page 71.

Two Fruits Meringue Pie
Serves 4–6

Pastry		
100 g	self-raising flour, sifted	4 oz
50 g	shredded suet	2 oz
15 ml spoon	caster sugar	1 tablespoon
1	egg, size 3, beaten	1
	a little milk, to mix	
Filling		
1	grapefruit, rind and juice	1
150 ml	crushed pineapple *or*	¼ pint
	strong pineapple juice	
3 × 5 ml spoons	cornflour	3 teaspoons
150 g	caster sugar	6 oz
25 g	butter *or* margarine	1 oz
2	eggs, size 2, separated	2
	a little more caster sugar,	
	to sprinkle	

Method

1 First, make the pastry by mixing the flour, suet and sugar to a firm dough with the egg and milk. Roll out on a lightly floured surface and line a 18–20 cm/7–8 in. flan dish. Prick the base and bake blind for 15 minutes at 200°C/400°F/Gas Mark 6, removing the foil or paper and beans after 10 minutes (see page 12).

2 Meanwhile, put the rind and juice of the grapefruit into a pan with the pineapple. There should be about 250 ml/½ pint of thick liquid. If not, make up to this amount with water. Bring to the boil. Blend the cornflour with a little cold water and slowly add the juice to it, stirring all the time. Return to the pan, bring back to the boil stirring until thickened.

3 Add 50 g/2 oz of the sugar and the butter and simmer

for two minutes. Remove from the heat and allow to cool slightly, then stir in the separated egg yolks. Pour into the baked flan case.

4 In a large, very clean bowl, whisk the egg whites until they form soft, firm peaks. Gradually whisk in the remaining 100 g/4 oz of sugar, a tablespoon at a time. The mixture should get stiffer and more shiny as you whisk.

5 Pile on top of the fruit mixture in the flan and swirl round with a knife to form attractive peaks. Sprinkle with a little extra sugar which gives the meringue a sparkle when baked.

6 Return to the oven at 180°C/350°F/Gas Mark 4 for a further 30 minutes until the meringue is pale golden and crisp. Serve hot or cold, with cream.

Prune and Orange Layer Pudding
Serves 4–6   (picture on page 59)

15 ml spoon	honey	1 tablespoon
250 g	self-raising flour, sifted	8 oz
125 g	shredded suet	4 oz
1	orange, rind of whole, and juice of half	1
	water, to mix	
439 g can (or 150 g)	prunes, drained and pitted (or dried and cooked)	15½ oz can (or 6 oz)
3–4 × 15 ml spoons	caster sugar	3–4 table-spoons

Method

1 First, grease a 0.85 litre/1½ pint pudding basin and put the honey in the base.

2 Cut the pith from the unsqueezed orange half, then cut into rings. Arrange a small whole ring in the centre, cut the others in half and place around the central one.

3 When the prunes are prepared, make the suet pastry up, by mixing the rind in with the suet, flour and juice and using extra water, if necessary. Mix to a stiff dough.

4 Divide the dough into four, not quite equal, pieces, as the top of the basin is obviously larger than the base. Roll out each piece to a round to fit approximately.

5 Place the smallest round on top of the orange rings, press gently to fit to the sides of the basin. Layer with a third of the prunes. Cover with some sugar, then another pastry layer. Continue with layers, ending with the largest suet round at the top.

6 Cover with greased and pleated (see page 14) greaseproof paper and foil. Press the edges under to seal and steam for two hours. Leave to stand for 5 minutes before turning out. Serve with custard or cream.

NB If you use dried prunes in this recipe, soak them overnight and cook in the same water for 10 minutes with sugar to sweeten.

Pear and Ginger Pudding
Makes one 1.1 litre/2 pint basin

50 g	butter, softened	2 oz
125 g	soft brown sugar	5 oz
125 g	fresh white breadcrumbs	5 oz
50 g	shredded suet	2 oz
500 g	hard pears, such as Conference	1 lb
1	lemon, rind only	1
25 g	preserved stem ginger, chopped	1 oz
2	eggs, size 2, beaten	2

Method

1 Mix the butter and 50 g/2 oz of the sugar together in a 1.1 litre/2 pint basin, then spread around the sides and base. Press about 25 g/1 oz of breadcrumbs round the basin too.

2 Mix the rest of the crumbs with the suet.

3 Peel and grate the pears and add the lemon rind, chopped stem ginger, remaining sugar and eggs.

4 Press a third of the breadcrumb mixture on the base of the basin, top with half the pears. Repeat the layers finishing with the breadcrumbs.

5 Cover with pleated, greased greaseproof paper and

Spotted Dick (p. 56), Pear and ginger pudding, Rich rice pudding (p. 62)

double thickness of foil (see page 14) and steam or boil for 2 hours. Serve hot, turned out, with a sweet, white sauce (see page 70) flavoured with some of the syrup from the stem ginger jar.

Spotted Dick Pudding
Serves 3–4

100 g	self-raising flour	4 oz
	pinch of salt	
50 g	shredded suet	2 oz
40 g	caster sugar	1½ oz
50 g	currants	2 oz
25 g	mixed peel	1 oz
1	egg, size 3, beaten	1
4 × 15 ml spoons	milk	4 tablespoons

Method
1 Mix together the dry ingredients.
2 Add the egg and sufficient milk to produce a smooth dropping consistency.
3 Transfer the mixture to a greased 0.55 litre/1 pint pudding basin.
4 Cover with pleated greased greaseproof paper and foil (see page 14) and steam for 1½–2 hours.
5 Turn out and serve hot with syrup sauce and/or custard.

Syrup Sauce

4 × 15 ml spoons	golden syrup	4 tablespoons
2 × 15 ml spoons	water	2 tablespoons
	juice of ½ lemon	

Method
1 Bring the syrup and water to the boil in a small saucepan.
2 Stir in lemon juice and serve.

NB This pudding can be baked in a traditional long roly-poly tin as in the photograph on page 55, but you would need to double or treble the mixture, depending on the size of the tin, and bake at 180°C/350°F/Gas Mark 4 for about 1 hour.

Cumberland Pudding (picture on front cover)
Serves 4–6

75 g	self-raising flour	3 oz
75 g	fresh white breadcrumbs	3 oz
75 g	shredded suet	3 oz
	pinch of salt	
75 g	soft brown sugar	3 oz
1	lemon, grated rind only	1
1	large cooking apple, peeled, cored and finely chopped	1
15 ml spoon	syrup *or* treacle	1 tablespoon
2	eggs, size 3, beaten	2

Method
1 Mix together the flour, breadcrumbs, suet, salt, sugar and lemon rind.
2 Stir in the apple, syrup and eggs and mix thoroughly.
3 Transfer the mixture to a greased 0.85 litre/1½ pint pudding basin.
4 Cover with pleated greased greaseproof paper and foil (see page 14) and steam for 2 hours.
5 Turn out and serve hot with custard, cream or the soured cream sauce on page 71.

Butterscotch Banana Pudding
Serves 6

Topping		
50 g	butter, softened	2 oz
50 g	soft brown sugar	2 oz
Pudding		
75 g	self-raising flour, sifted	3 oz
75 g	fresh white breadcrumbs	3 oz
50 g	soft brown sugar	2 oz
75 g	shredded suet	3 oz
	a little ground nutmeg	
2	bananas, 1 sliced thinly, 1 mashed	2
1	egg, size 3, beaten	1
	milk, to mix	

Method

1 Cream the butter and sugar in a 0.85 litre/1½ pint pudding basin and then spread around the base and sides to coat evenly.

2 Arrange the slices of one banana around the bowl by sticking them to the creamed mixture.

3 Mix the flour, breadcrumbs, sugar, suet and nutmeg together. Beat the mashed banana with the egg and mix in, adding extra milk if necessary to form a soft dropping consistency. Spoon into the prepared bowl, leaving a row of sliced banana uncovered so that the mixture will expand onto it.

4 Cover with pleated greased greaseproof paper and foil (see page 14), and steam for 2 hours.

5 Allow to stand for 5 minutes, then turn out onto a serving plate.

Little Lemon Honey Pots
Makes 4

If you have the time, make four lemon butterflies with two slices of lemon, and put them on the base of the cups before cooking these little puds.

4 × 5 ml spoons	honey, for tops of puddings	4 teaspoons
75 g	fresh white breadcrumbs	3 oz
75 g	self-raising flour, sifted	3 oz
75 g	shredded suet	3 oz
6 × 15 ml spoons	honey, warmed slightly	6 tablespoons
1	lemon, rind and juice	1
1	egg, size 2, beaten	1

Method

1 Grease four teacups or darioles well, then put a teaspoonful of honey at the bottom of each.

2 Mix all the other ingredients together and divide between the cups.

Apple beehives (p. 68), Prune and orange layer pudding (p. 53), Little lemon honey pots

3 Place a small greased greaseproof paper disc lightly on top of each cup and cover with foil, pleated to allow room for expansion (see page 14).

4 Steam for 1 hour, then turn out onto individual sweet dishes or one platter and serve hot with cream or custard.

NB Can be made as one larger pudding in a 0.85 litre/1½ pint basin and steamed for 2 hours. Substitute golden syrup for honey in a syrup pudding, and 75 g/3 oz caster sugar plus 2 × 15 ml spoons/2 tablespoons jam for the top in a jam pudding (picture on page 63).

Father's Stout and Mincemeat Roll
Serves 6

150 g	self-raising flour, sifted	6 oz
75 g	shredded suet	3 oz
	pinch of salt	
about 6 × 15 ml spoons	stout *or* beer	about 6 tablespoons
250 g	mincemeat, homemade *or* bought	8 oz
1	medium cooking apple, peeled and thinly sliced	1

Method

1 Mix the flour, suet and salt with enough stout to make a firm dough. Roll this out on a lightly floured surface to a large neat rectangle about 5 mm/¼ in. thick.

2 Spread the mincemeat over the pastry and arrange the apple slices on top.

3 Roll up and cut the edges, if necessary, to neaten.

4 Place on a sheet of greased greaseproof paper and enclose fairly loosely, then overwrap in a large piece of foil, again quite loosely to allow room for expansion. Make sure the ends and join of the foil are well folded to seal so that the roll does not get wet.

5 Steam or boil for an hour and a half until cooked, then turn out onto a warmed plate and serve hot with custard.

NB This pudding can also be baked at 180°C/350°F/Gas Mark 4 for about 30 minutes, but do not cover.

Bread Pudding
Serves 6–8

250 ml	milk	½ pint
250 g	stale white *or* brown breadcrumbs	8 oz
50 g	currants	2 oz
50 g	sultanas	2 oz
50 g	mixed peel	2 oz
50 g	sugar	2 oz
50 g	shredded suet	2 oz
2 × 5 ml spoons	mixed spice	2 teaspoons
1	egg, size 3, beaten with a little milk	1

Method

1 Pour the milk over the breadcrumbs and leave to soak for 30 minutes.

2 Mix in the currants, sultanas, peel, sugar, suet and spice.

3 Add the beaten egg and milk and beat well.

4 Pour the mixture into a greased small roasting tin and bake at 180°C/350°F/Gas Mark 4 for 1½ hours or until firm and golden.

5 Sprinkle with caster sugar, if liked, before serving.

Apple and Cranberry Charlotte (picture on page 67)
Serves 4–6

500 g	cooking apples, peeled and chopped	1 lb
100 g	sugar	4 oz
75 g	shredded suet	3 oz
250 g	fresh breadcrumbs, brown *or* white	8 oz
4 × 15 ml spoons	cranberry sauce	4 tablespoons

Method

1 Mix the apples and sugar together.

2 Mix the suet with 175 g/6 oz of the breadcrumbs and press a layer into the base of a greased pie or ovenproof dish.

3 Sprinkle with a layer of apple and dot with cranberry

sauce, using just over a tablespoon. Continue with the layers of breadcrumbs, apple and cranberry sauce finishing with fruit. Then sprinkle on the remaining unmixed breadcrumbs and bake at 180°C/350°F/Gas Mark 4 for about 45 minutes until golden on top. Serve hot with custard or cream.

Chocolate and Black Cherry Loaf (picture on page 67)
Serves 4–6

75 g	self-raising flour, sifted	3 oz
25 g	cocoa	1 oz
75 g	fresh white breadcrumbs	3 oz
75 g	shredded suet	3 oz
50 g	soft brown sugar	2 oz
2 × 15 ml spoons	golden syrup, warmed slightly	2 tablespoons
2	eggs, size 3, beaten a little milk, if needed	2
425 g can	black cherries, stoned and drained	15 oz can

Method
1 First, grease a 500 g/1 lb loaf tin and line the base with greased greaseproof paper.
2 Sift the flour and cocoa together, then mix in the rest of the ingredients using half the cherries and adding enough milk to make a soft dropping consistency.
3 Turn into the loaf tin and bake at 180°C/350°F/Gas Mark 4 for about 1 hour until cooked and risen. Allow to stand for a few minutes, then turn out onto a warmed serving dish and serve with the remaining cherries and cream or a soured cream sauce (see page 71).

Rich Rice Pudding (picture on page 55)
Serves 4–6

Victorian cooks would often add a spoonful of suet to enrich a rice pudding, an idea well worth while trying when next you make one.

Bread pudding (p. 61), Father's stout and mincemeat roll (p. 60), Traditional jam steamed pudding (p. 60)

75 g	short grain pudding rice, washed	3 oz
25 g	light soft brown sugar	1 oz
1.25 ml spoon	nutmeg	¼ teaspoon
700 ml	milk	1¼ pints
150 ml	evaporated milk, undiluted	¼ pint
25 g	sultanas, optional	1 oz
15 ml spoon	shredded suet	1 tablespoon

Method
1 Put the rice in a greased pie dish with all the other ingredients and sprinkle on the suet.
2 Bake at 160°C/325°F/Gas Mark 3 for 2–2½ hours until golden on top and creamy inside. Serve hot.

Rhubarb and Mallow Flan (picture on page 51)
Serves 6

Base		
150 g	self-raising flour, sifted	6 oz
75 g	shredded suet	3 oz
25 g	caster sugar	1 oz
1	egg, size 3, beaten	1
	milk, to mix	
Filling		
500 g	rhubarb, chopped into 2 cm/1 in. lengths	1 lb
50 g	sugar	2 oz
	a little water	
Topping		
100 g	white and pink marsh-mallows	4 oz

Method
1 Preheat the oven to 190°C/375°F/Gas Mark 5.
2 Mix the base ingredients together using enough egg and milk to make a soft firm dough. Roll out on a lightly floured surface to fit a 20 cm/8 in. flan dish.
3 Bake blind (see page 12) for 10 minutes, then remove the paper and beans or foil and return to the oven for a further 5 minutes.

4 Meanwhile, prepare and gently stew the rhubarb until soft with the sugar and just enough water to prevent the fruit from sticking to the pan.

5 Spoon into the flan case, draining any excess juice.

6 Arrange the marshmallows on top of the rhubarb. Return to the oven for about 10 minutes until the marshmallows have melted. Serve hot or cold.

Strawberry Cream Cake (picture on page 51)
Serves 4–6

Base		
50 g	self-raising flour, sifted	2 oz
25 g	shredded suet	1 oz
40 g	caster sugar	1½ oz
50 g	ground almonds	2 oz
5 ml spoon	almond essence	1 teaspoon
1	egg, size 3, beaten	1
Topping		
75 g	cream cheese, softened	3 oz
15 ml spoon	caster sugar	1 tablespoon
2 × 5 ml spoons	lemon juice	2 teaspoons
250 g	fresh strawberries, hulled and halved	8 oz
3–4 × 15 ml spoons	redcurrant jelly, melted and rubbed through a sieve	3–4 tablespoons

Method

1 Mix the base ingredients together, using enough beaten egg to make a soft dough. Press and mould into the base of a 20 cm/8 in. flan dish using your knuckles. Bake at 190°C/375°F/Gas Mark 5 for 20 minutes until golden and firm.

2 Beat the cream cheese with the sugar and lemon juice and prepare the strawberries and redcurrant jelly.

3 When the base is done, turn out if liked, or allow to cool and serve in the flan dish.

4 Spread the cooled base with the cream cheese, top with the halved strawberries and coat with the melted warm redcurrant jelly. Allow the jelly glaze to set and serve chilled.

Apricot and Almond Upside Down Cake
Serves 4–6

2 × 15 ml spoons	honey *or* golden syrup, warmed	2 tablespoons
425 g can	apricot halves, drained	15 oz can
100 g	self-raising flour, sifted	4 oz
50 g	shredded suet	2 oz
50 g	caster sugar	2 oz
75 g	ground almonds	3 oz
5 ml spoon	almond essence	1 teaspoon
1	egg, size 3, beaten	1
	milk, to mix	
	some toasted whole blanched almonds, to decorate	

Method
1 Lightly grease a 18–20 cm/7–8 in. sandwich tin and spoon in the warmed honey or syrup.
2 Arrange the apricot halves, cut side down, on top of the syrup so that when the cake is turned out the hollows of the apricots will face up.
3 Mix the rest of the ingredients together, adding enough milk to make a soft dropping consistency. Spoon on top of the apricots and level slightly.
4 Bake at 190°C/375°F/Gas Mark 5 for about 25 minutes until risen and golden. Turn out and fill each hollow of the apricots with a toasted almond. Serve hot with cream.

Date 'n Nutty Doughnuts (picture on front cover)
Makes 12

Another surprising but simple use for a suet shortcut dough is deep fried doughnuts. This recipe has a spicy, nutty filling, but you could also use it to wrap up small pieces of fruit such as canned apricots, pineapple, banana or even red jam!

Apricot and almond upside down cake, Apple and cranberry charlotte (p. 61), Chocolate and black cherry loaf (p. 62)

Dough

150 g	self-raising flour, sifted	6 oz
75 g	shredded suet	3 oz
25 g	caster sugar	1 oz
1	egg, size 3, beaten	1
	milk, to bind	

Filling

25 g	butter, softened	1 oz
2 × 5 ml spoons	soft brown sugar	2 teaspoons
40 g	dates, chopped	1½ oz
25 g	walnuts, chopped	1 oz
1.25 ml spoon	mixed spice	¼ teaspoon
	vegetable oil, for deep frying	
	caster sugar, to toss in	

Method

1 Mix the flour, suet and sugar together, then bind to a stiff dough with the egg, adding milk if required.

2 Roll out the dough on a lightly floured surface to about 5 mm/¼ in. thick and cut into 12 × 5 cm/2 in. rounds, re-rolling if necessary.

3 Lightly brush the edges with water.

4 Cream the butter and sugar together and mix with the filling ingredients. Divide between the dough rounds.

5 Draw the edges in, enclosing the filling, pressing well together to seal.

6 Heat sufficient clean vegetable oil to come half way up the sides of a deep chip pan, until 185°C/360°F or a small piece of crustless bread browns in 45 seconds.

7 Carefully fry four to six doughnuts at a time until golden brown, about 5 minutes, then drain on kitchen paper.

8 Toss in caster sugar whilst hot and serve warm or cold, with the apricot sauce on page 70, or the syrup sauce on page 56.

Apple Beehives (picture on page 59)
Makes 4

Simple, spicy apple dumplings which are super served hot with cream or custard.

Pastry

250 g	self-raising flour, sifted	8 oz
125 g	shredded suet	4 oz
2.5 ml spoon	salt	½ teaspoon
1	egg, size 3, beaten	1
	water, to mix	

Filling

4	medium-size cooking apples, peeled and cored	4
50 g	soft brown sugar	2 oz
50 g	dried mixed fruit	2 oz
5 ml spoon	mixed spice	1 teaspoon
25 g	butter	1 oz
1	egg, size 3, beaten, to glaze	1

Method

1 Mix the pastry ingredients together, with extra water if necessary, to make a firm dough.

2 Roll out to a long oblong 5 mm/¼ in. thick and cut into four 1 cm/½ in. strips long enough to wind round the apples.

3 Mix the sugar, fruit and spice together and spoon into each apple core cavity. Dot with butter.

4 Starting at the top, wind the pastry strip round each apple, overlapping slightly as you wind. Damp and seal the joins securely.

5 Re-roll the trimmings and cut out eight pastry leaves. Fix these to the top.

6 Place on a greased baking tray, glaze with egg and bake for 15 minutes at 200°C/400°F/Gas Mark 6, reducing to 180°C/350°F/Gas Mark 4 for a further 25–30 minutes.

SOME SIMPLE SWEET SAUCES

Crème Anglais (or, Real Custard Sauce)

This is perhaps my favourite sweet sauce, and well worth the time spent stirring and stirring. It is not as thick as we have now come to expect custard to be, more the consistency of pouring cream.

3	egg yolks	3
250 ml	milk	½ pint
1–2 × 15 ml spoons	caster sugar	1–2 tablespoons
	few drops vanilla essence	

Method

1 Beat the egg yolks in a medium-size bowl with 2 × 15 ml spoons/2 tablespoons of milk.

2 Heat the rest of the milk with the sugar and vanilla essence and bring to the boil.

3 Pour from a height onto the eggs, stirring vigorously. Then pour back, through a sieve, into the saucepan.

4 Using a wooden spoon, and over the lowest heat possible, stir continuously until the sauce thickens slightly and coats the back of the spoon. To tell when this stage is reached, draw your finger down the back of the spoon, if there is a definite parting, the sauce is ready. Pour into a sauceboat and cover until ready to serve. This sauce is nice hot or cold.

NB The danger of overheating and curdling this sauce is great. If you don't trust yourself or your cooker, stir the sauce in a basin over a pan of gently simmering water. If you get tiny lumps appearing, remove from the heat immediately and plunge the pan or basin into a bowl of very cold water. It may be as well to have one standing by!

Apricot Sauce

Heat an equal number of 15 ml spoons/tablespoons of apricot jam and water with a good squeeze of lemon juice. Strain through a sieve into a sauceboat and add some chopped almonds, if liked.

Sweet White Sauce

Mix a 15 ml spoon/1 tablespoon of cornflour to a smooth paste with a little milk taken from 250 ml/½ pint. Put the rest to heat and bring to the boil. Pour onto the cornflour paste, stirring, then pour back into the pan, still stirring. Bring to the boil again and add 15 g/½ oz butter and sugar to taste, about 1–2 × 15 ml spoons/1–2 tablespoons. Simmer for a minute then pour into a sauceboat and cover until ready to serve. If liked, add a little brandy, rum or vanilla essence, especially for Christmas pudding.

Rich Chocolate Sauce
Melt very gently a 100 g/3½ oz bar of plain chocolate broken into pieces with 150 ml/¼ pint of water and a 15 ml spoon/1 tablespoon of golden syrup. Add extra flavouring as desired such as brandy, grated orange, coffee essence or stir in 15 g/½ oz butter just before serving.

Brandy Butter/Brandy Hard Sauce
Cream 100 g/4 oz of unsalted butter until light and fluffy, then beat in 100 g/4 oz each of sifted icing sugar and caster sugar and 50 g/2 oz ground almonds. Flavour with 2 × 15 ml spoons/2 tablespoons of brandy (or rum) and perhaps a little nutmeg.

Soured Cream Sauce
Blend a 150 g/6 fl oz carton of soured cream, 3 × 15 ml spoons/3 tablespoons of whipped cream, 2 × 15 ml spoons/2 tablespoons of caster sugar, rind and juice of a lemon, pinch mixed spice all thoroughly together and serve with hot steamed puddings and sweet pies.

Butterscotch Sauce
Slowly melt 25 g/1 oz of salted butter with 100 g/4 oz soft brown sugar. Add 150 ml/¼ pint water and stirring, heat gently until the sugar dissolves. In a cup, blend a 15 ml spoon/1 tablespoon of cornflour to a smooth paste, add a little of the hot liquid to the cup, then return to the pan, stirring until thickened. Add a few drops of vanilla essence, simmer for two minutes, then serve hot.

Bakes

Chocolate Caramel Bars
Makes 12–14

This should be a sure fire winner with children because it combines two of their favourite flavours, caramel and chocolate on a nice plain cake base, quickly made with suet.

Base		
100 g	self-raising flour, sifted	4 oz
50 g	shredded suet	2 oz
25 g	light soft brown sugar	1 oz
1	egg, size 3, beaten	1
	extra milk, if necessary	

Filling		
196 g tin (small size)	sweetened condensed milk	7 oz tin (small size)
100 g	margarine	4 oz
50 g	sugar	2 oz
2 × 10 ml spoons	golden syrup	2 dessert-spoons

Topping		
250 g	cooking chocolate, plain *or* milk	8 oz

Method
1 Mix the flour, suet, sugar, egg and extra milk, if necessary, to a firm soft dough, then press into a greased square or rectangular cake tin, with the base lined with greased greaseproof paper.
2 Bake at 180°C/350°F/Gas Mark 4 for 20–25 minutes until golden and cooked. Allow to cool in the tin.
3 Meanwhile, heat the filling ingredients together till melted, then bring to the boil and boil for 5 minutes, stirring occasionally to prevent the pan from burning. Remove from the heat and beat well until thickened

then pour onto the base and allow to get quite cold and solid.

4 When cold, melt the chocolate very slowly over hot water (not too hot though, or the chocolate will go lumpy). Beat the melted chocolate until smooth.

5 Pour onto the caramel, smoothing over with a palette knife dipped in hot water, if necessary. Allow the chocolate to set slightly, then mark into fingers. Turn the lot out when completely set. Cut up into fingers with a large sharp knife.

Peanut and Orange Jacks
Makes about 24

There was a theory circulating some years ago that peanuts contained all the nourishment a body needed except Vitamin C, and an orange a day would balance that up. If so, then these nutty, oaty biscuits are highly nutritious and a perfect tea-time treat for your children. They also taste quite good!

100 g	salted peanuts, finely chopped	4 oz
100 g	flaked porridge oats	4 oz
100 g	shredded suet	4 oz
100 g	self-raising flour	4 oz
1	orange, rind of whole and juice of half	1
1	egg, size 3, beaten	1
Icing		
100 g	icing sugar, sifted juice of half an orange warm water, if necessary	4 oz
about 24	whole peanuts, to decorate	about 24

Method

1 Mix all the biscuit ingredients together to a firm dough. Roll out to about 5 mm/¼ in. thick and cut out as many biscuits as possible, using a 5 cm/2 in. cutter and re-rolling as necessary. It may be better to do this in batches as each lot cooks.

2 Bake on a lightly greased baking sheet at 190°C/375°F/

Gas Mark 5 for 10–15 minutes until a golden brown on the edges and firm to the touch.

3 Scoop off immediately with a palette knife onto a cooling tray and leave to crisp up.

4 When cool, mix the icing sugar with the orange juice and just enough water until it is the consistency of runny honey.

5 Put a scant teaspoonful of icing in the centre of each biscuit and top with a peanut. If possible, eat on the day of baking, as the moisture in the icing could be absorbed by the biscuit and become soggy.

Singing Hinnies
Makes about 20 small ones or one large one

I think this is the nicest name of all our regional recipes and I'm sure all those from the north east will whole-heartedly agree. Hinnie is their term for 'love' or 'dear', most often applied to women. And as for the first part of the name – these little cakes really do seem to sing, as they sizzle away.

350 g	self-raising flour, sifted	12 oz
50 g	ground rice *or* semolina	2 oz
50 g	caster sugar	2 oz
25 g	shredded suet	1 oz
5 ml spoon	salt	1 teaspoon
75 g	currants	3 oz
approx. 200 ml	top of the milk	approx. 7 fl oz

Method

1 Mix all the dry ingredients together, then add enough milk to mix to a firm soft dough.

2 Heat a griddle or large heavy frying pan and grease lightly.

3 Roll the mixture out to about 5 mm/¼ in. thick to either fit the pan or griddle if you wish to make a large one, or cut out in 5 cm/2 in. rounds, re-rolling as necessary.

Singing hinnies, Chocolate caramel bars (p. 72), Malted fruit loaf (p. 76), Peanut and orange jacks (p. 73)

4 Cook gently until browned, then turn over and cook the other side. Serve them warm, split and buttered.

Malted Fruit Loaf

Makes 1 large *or* 2 small loaves

A good, wholesome, easy-to-make tea bread. Leave it for a day in a tin before cutting, then serve thinly sliced and buttered.

250 g	self-raising flour	10 oz
2.5 ml spoon	salt	½ teaspoon
1.25 ml spoon	bicarbonate of soda	¼ teaspoon
50 g	soft brown sugar	2 oz
150 g	sultanas	6 oz
50 g	shredded suet	2 oz
125 ml	milk	¼ pint
15 ml spoon	malt extract	1 tablespoon
15 ml spoon	golden syrup *or* black treacle	1 tablespoon
2 × 5 ml spoons	caster sugar, to sprinkle	2 teaspoons

Method
1 Pre-heat the oven to 180°C/350°F/Gas Mark 4.
2 Sift the flour, salt and soda, then add the sugar, fruit and suet. Mix well.
3 Warm the milk, malt and syrup or treacle in a pan and allow to cool.
4 Mix the liquid in with the dry ingredients and turn into either a greased and lined 1 kg/2 lb loaf tin or two ½ kg/1 lb tins. Sprinkle the extra sugar on top.
5 Bake the small tins for about 45 minutes and the large tin for about 65 minutes.

Suppers and Snacks

Meatza Pizza Pie
Serves 4–6

If you find mozzarella cheese difficult to track down, then use slices of the quick melting mild Lancashire cheese, or even Edam.

Pastry base		
250 g	self-raising flour, sifted	8 oz
125 g	shredded suet	4 oz
1	egg, size 3, beaten	1
	water, to mix	
Topping		
250 g	minced beef	8 oz
1	clove garlic, crushed	1
2 × 15 ml spoons	olive *or* corn oil	2 tablespoons
425 g can	peeled tomatoes	15 oz can
5 ml spoon	dried oregano *or* marjoram	1 teaspoon
	salt and ground black pepper	
250 g	mozzarella cheese, sliced	8 oz
2	tomatoes, sliced, optional	2
	dried oregano, to sprinkle	

Method

1 Make up the shortcut pastry (see page 7) binding with the egg and adding extra water if necessary to make a firm dough.
2 Roll out and line a medium size roasting pan or Swiss roll tin. Bake blind (see page 12) at 200°C/400°F/Gas Mark 6 for 15 minutes, removing the foil or baking beans and paper after 10 minutes.
3 Meanwhile, fry the beef and garlic in the oil until browned, then add the canned tomatoes, herbs and seasonings. Cook until almost all the liquid has evaporated away, about 15–20 minutes.
4 Spoon into the flan case and arrange the cheese on

top. Sprinkle with more herbs (or even top with slices of fresh tomato, if to hand), then return to the oven until the cheese has melted. Serve hot, cut into slices.

Pissaladière
Serves 3–4

Base

150 g	self-raising flour, sifted	6 oz
75 g	shredded suet	3 oz
1	egg, size 3, beaten	1
	pinch of salt	
	milk, to mix	

Filling

1	large onion, sliced in rings	1
2	cloves garlic, crushed	2
3 × 15 ml spoons	olive *or* vegetable oil	3 tablespoons
425 g can	peeled tomatoes	15 oz can
5 ml spoon	mixed dried herbs,	1 teaspoon
5 ml spoon	sugar	1 teaspoon
	salt and ground black pepper	

Topping

64 g can	anchovy fillets, drained	2¼ oz can
about 10	black olives, stoned	about 10

Method

1 Mix the flour, suet, egg, salt and enough milk to make a stiff dough. Roll out and line a 20 cm/8 in. flan dish. Bake blind (see page 12) at 200°C/400°F/Gas Mark 6 for 10 minutes, then remove the paper and beans or foil and return to the oven for a further 5 minutes.

2 Meanwhile, fry the onion and garlic in the oil until soft and transparent (about 10 minutes) then add the tomatoes, herbs, sugar and seasoning. Mash the tomatoes and cook for a further 10–15 minutes until pulpy.

3 Spoon into the flan case. Cut the anchovies in half lengthways and arrange in a lattice pattern on top, then arrange the olives in the lattice. Serve hot or cold.

Meatza pizza pie (p. 77), Pissaladière

Saucy Sausage Slice
Serves 4–6

A sausage and egg pie is always a good midweek meal to satisfy your budget *and* the family's appetite. This is perhaps a more interesting version with a light shortcut pastry that is almost a cheat's flaky pastry.

Pastry		
250 g	self-raising flour, sifted	8 oz
125 g	shredded suet	4 oz
1	egg, size 3, beaten	1
	pinch of salt	
	extra milk to mix, if needed	
Filling		
500 g	sausagemeat	1 lb
4 × 15 ml spoons	fruity sauce *or* pickle	4 tablespoons
3	eggs, hard boiled and quartered	3
2.5 ml spoon	dried rubbed sage	½ teaspoon
100 g	Cheddar cheese, sliced	4 oz
	a little beaten egg *or* milk to glaze	

Method

1 Make the pastry by mixing the ingredients together with egg and enough milk for a firm, soft dough. Roll out on a lightly floured surface to a large rectangle 5 mm/¼ in. thick. Cut this in two.

2 Place one half on a greased baking sheet and spread with the sausagemeat to within 1 cm/½ in. of the edges. Use floured hands to pat out the sausagemeat first, if necessary.

3 Spread with fruity sauce or pickle and top with the hard boiled eggs. Sprinkle on the sage and cover with the slices of cheese.

4 Damp the edges and cover with the other half of the pastry. Seal, trim and crimp the edges. Cut slits down the centre with a sharp knife or kitchen scissors.

5 Glaze and bake at 200°C/400°F/Gas Mark 6 for 15 minutes, then lower the heat to 180°C/350°F/Gas Mark 4 for a further 20 minutes. Serve hot, sliced, with tomatoes and salad.

Bird's Nests (picture on page 87)
Serves 4

I came across this recipe in a handwritten family cookery book of 1887 and yet it is just the sort of dish to serve these days for a light salad lunch or picnic. It has a herby forcemeat coating round hard boiled eggs, similar to Scotch eggs. Do take care though when deep frying and follow the temperature guides exactly. The secret of successful deep fat frying lies in getting the right temperature to begin with – too low and the eggs could break up.

6	eggs, size 3	6
100 g	fresh white breadcrumbs	4 oz
1	lemon, rind and juice	1
3 × 15 ml spoons	fresh chopped chives (*or* half quantity of dried)	3 tablespoons
4 × 15 ml spoons	fresh chopped parsley	4 tablespoons
50 g	shredded suet	2 oz
	salt and ground black pepper	
	dried breadcrumbs, to coat	
	vegetable oil for deep frying	

Method
1 First, hard boil four eggs, then immediately plunge into cold water to prevent a dark ring forming around them.
2 When quite cold, shell, wash, dry and dust with a little flour.
3 Mix the fresh breadcrumbs with the lemon rind and juice, herbs, suet and one beaten egg, then season well.
4 Divide in four and press around each floured egg.
5 Beat the remaining egg and dip each coated egg in it, then into the dried breadcrumbs. For complete success, dip and coat each egg at one time, then place on a plate ready for frying.
6 Fill a deep fat frying pan one half full of clean vegetable oil and heat to 190°C/375°F, or until a small piece of crustless bread browns in 30 seconds.

7 Carefully lower the eggs into the fat in a chip basket or with a draining spoon. For best results fry only two together each time. When golden brown, about 5 minutes, drain on kitchen paper. Cut each egg in half to serve, and eat warm or cold with salad.

Quickie Can Can Cobbler
Serves 4–6 children

A quick, protein-packed, children's favourite with little gooey cheese cubes.

425 g can	baked beans	15 oz can
425 g can	frankfurter sausages, drained and chopped	15 oz can
100 g	Cheddar cheese pinch dried mixed herbs	4 oz
100 g	self-raising flour, sifted	4 oz
50 g	shredded suet	2 oz
5 ml spoon	dry mustard powder salt and ground black pepper milk, to mix	1 teaspoon
2	large tomatoes, sliced thinly	2

Method
1 Empty the baked beans and sausages into a 0.85 litre/ 1½ pint pie dish. If the beans look as if they are rather 'saucy' then scoop out some of the excess sauce.
2 Cut 50 g/2 oz of the cheese into small cubes and stir into the pie dish. Sprinkle on a pinch of herbs and season.
3 Grate the remaining cheese and mix with the flour, suet, mustard powder, seasoning and milk to a soft, firm dough. Roll out on a lightly floured board to 5 mm/ ¼ in. thick. Cut out about 12 × 4 cm/1½ in. rounds, re-rolling as necessary.
4 Arrange the scone rounds on top of the pie dish

Saucy sausage slice (p. 80), Quickie can can cobbler

alternating with the slices of tomato. Brush the tops with milk and bake at 200°C/400°F/Gas Mark 6 for 20–25 minutes until golden brown and risen. Serve hot with cabbage or another green leafy vegetable.

Noughts and Crosses (picture on page 11)

Cocktail drinks and parties are fast coming back into fashion as entertaining gets more expensive and food costs soar. But that's no excuse for serving no food at all, or sticking to crisps and nuts. Hand round a plateful of these hot, homemade cocktail nibbles to act as tasty blotting paper. Your guests could even play a quick game of noughts and crosses with them first!

150 g	self-raising flour, sifted	6 oz
75 g	shredded suet	3 oz
1	egg, size 3, beaten	1
	water, to mix	
Filling		
75 g	cream cheese, softened	3 oz
3 × 5 ml spoons	anchovy paste (Patum Peperium)	3 teaspoons
	cayenne pepper, optional	
1	egg, size 3, beaten with a little anchovy essence	1
65 g can	anchovy fillets	2¼ oz can
	a few stuffed olives	

Method
1 Mix the flour and suet to a firm dough with the egg and extra water if necessary. Roll out on a lightly floured board to a large rectangle 5 mm/¼ in. thick. Cut into half.
2 Beat the cream cheese and anchovy paste until creamy, adding a pinch of cayenne if liked.
3 Spread the cream cheese mixture on one side of the pastry halves, top with the other and press down well. Cut into small squares.
4 Place on greased baking sheets and glaze with the egg beaten with anchovy essence.

5 Drain the anchovy fillets, cut in half lengthways, then cut into small strips. Slice the olives into rounds. Make crosses with the anchovy strips and noughts with the olive slices, on top of each glazed square.

6 Bake at 200°C/400°F/Gas Mark 6 for 15 minutes until golden and crisp. Serve warm.

Beefburger Pasties
Makes 4

Most bought packet pasties are a bit thin on meat filling, and homemade ones can take some time to make. So, here is a compromise using just a small packet of frozen beefburgers, and of course, a quick shortcut pastry.

Pastry		
100 g	self-raising flour, sifted	4 oz
50 g	shredded suet	2 oz
	pinch of salt	
I	egg, size 3, beaten	I
	water, to mix	
Filling		
2 × 56 g	beefburgers, thawed if frozen	2 × 2 oz
50 g	canned mixed vegetables *or* thawed frozen casserole vegetables	2 oz
	salt and ground black pepper	
	beaten egg, to glaze	

Method
1 Make up the shortcut pastry until you have a firm dough, using extra water if necessary, and roll out to 5 mm/¼ in. thick on a lightly floured surface. Using a large saucer as a guide, cut out four rounds, re-rolling as necessary. Damp the edges.

2 Cut the beefburgers in half and place on one side of each of the pastry rounds. Top with mixed vegetables and season.

3 Fold over the other half of pastry, seal and crimp edges. Glaze and bake at 200°C/400°F/Gas Mark 6 for 20–25 minutes or until golden and cooked. Serve hot.

Quick Steak and Kidney Pan Pudding
Serves 4

Good quality steak and kidney pie filling makes a most acceptable and economical main meal if stretched with some mushrooms to feed four. Add a speedy suet crust pastry which is cooked on top of the filling *in the pan* and you have a dish very similar to a steak and kidney pudding but cooked in a third of the time.

100 g	self-raising flour	4 oz
50 g	shredded suet	2 oz
	pinch of salt	
	pinch of dried herbs	
	water, to mix	
425 g can	steak and kidney pie filling	15 oz can
100 g	mushrooms, quartered	4 oz
2.5 ml spoon	dried thyme, optional	½ teaspoon
	Worcestershire sauce	

Method
1 Mix the flour, suet, salt and herbs to a firm dough with the water, then roll out on a lightly floured surface to a round to fit the size of saucepan you intend using.
2 Mix the pie filling with the mushrooms, thyme and a few dashes of Worcestershire sauce.
3 Place the dough on top of the meat, cover and cook gently for about 25 minutes.
4 Serve hot from the pan.

Hint The same quantity of suet crust can be used for a pan pudding with any pre-cooked sweet or savoury filling.

Beefburger pasties (p. 85), Sausage rolls (p. 10), Bird's nests (p. 81)

Festive Favourites

Christmas Pudding
Makes two 1.1 litre/2 pint puddings

I often make my puddings one year for the next as the flavours mature so beautifully, and I also find that a Christmas pudding brought out for a lunch on a cold summer Sunday is invariably greeted with delight.

225 g	shredded suet	8 oz
225 g	fresh breadcrumbs	8 oz
100 g	wholemeal flour	4 oz
225 g	soft brown sugar	8 oz
2.5 ml spoon	ground cloves	½ teaspoon
2.5 ml spoon	cinnamon	½ teaspoon
5 ml spoon	grated nutmeg	1 teaspoon
2.5 ml spoon	salt	½ teaspoon
300 g	currants	10 oz
300 g	sultanas	10 oz
225 g	large raisins *or* stoned dried prunes, chopped	8 oz
225 g	candied *or* mixed peel, chopped	8 oz
1	lemon, rind and juice	1
4	eggs, size 3, beaten	4
4 × 15 ml spoons	black treacle, warmed	4 tablespoons
150 ml	milk *or* stale ale	¼ pint
150 ml	brandy *or* rum	¼ pint

Method
1 Mix the suet with the breadcrumbs, flour, sugar, spices and salt in a very large bowl or even a very clean washing up bowl.
2 Add the dried fruit, peel, lemon rind and juice. Stir well.
3 Beat the eggs with the treacle, milk or ale and spirits and stir in thoroughly.
4 Divide between two 1.1 litre/2 pint bowls which have

been greased and the base lined with a disc of greased greaseproof paper.

5 Cover with pleated greased greaseproof paper and double thickness of foil (see page 14) and boil for a good 6 hours checking the water repeatedly. Re-cover when cold and store in a cool place until needed.

To serve

Boil for a further 4–6 hours. If you would prefer to have a lie in on Christmas morning, rather than get up to put the pudding on, then boil initially for 8 hours and re-boil for 2.

If you wish to flame the pudding, then warm two tablespoons of rum or brandy in a metal soup ladle and pour it over the pudding just as you are about to make your entrance. Do carry the pudding in with a cloth as the flaming spirit will make the dish very hot, and don't choose plastic holly if you intend flaming the pudding – it will melt all over the top. Serve with brandy hard sauce (page 71) and either cream, sweet white sauce (page 70), or real custard sauce (page 69).

To boil in a pudding cloth

If you want to make a Christmas pudding in the traditional spherical shape then use a large piece of pure cotton or linen sheet and boil the pudding suspended in a deep pan of water. You need the depth because the pudding should not touch the base of the pan, otherwise it will squash up a bit. Grease the cloth well, pile half the mixture in the centre and draw the cloth up around it. Allow a little room for expansion and tie securely with cotton string. Then tie the same string to a long handled wooden spoon or skewer and balance over the pan so the pudding hangs down inside the boiling water. Cover and boil as for a basin pudding. Interestingly enough, a turn of the century cookbook I have advises against this method in favour of the more 'modern' method of using a basin as some of the flavour is obviously lost in the water and certainly, the pudding is a lighter colour, but then the shape is perhaps more attractive.

Hint You can make a quick Christmas pudding with 500 g/1 lb mincemeat, 100 g/4 oz self-raising flour, 1 egg, 50 g/2 oz shredded suet and 15 ml spoon/1 tablespoon black treacle. Boil in a 0.85 litre/1½ pint basin for 2 hours.

Figgy Pudding
Makes one 1.1 litre/2 pint basin

Just the thing to offer festive carol singers.

225 g	dried figs, de-stalked and chopped	8 oz
150 g	fresh breadcrumbs	6 oz
50 g	self-raising flour	2 oz
100 g	shredded suet	4 oz
150 g	dark soft brown sugar	6 oz
75 g	sultanas	3 oz
50 g	candied *or* mixed peel, chopped	2 oz
50 g	almond flakes, lightly toasted	2 oz
2.5 ml spoon	ground nutmeg	½ teaspoon
	pinch of salt	
3	eggs, size 3, beaten	3
5 × 15 ml spoons	milk	5 tablespoons
5 × 15 ml spoons	sherry *or* brandy	5 tablespoons

Method
1 Mix all the dry ingredients together.
2 Beat the eggs with the milk and sherry or brandy.
3 Add the liquid to the dry ingredients and mix thoroughly.
4 Turn into a greased 1.1 litre/2 pint basin, with the base lined with a greased greaseproof paper disc.
5 Cover with pleated, greased greaseproof paper and double thickness of foil (see page 14) and steam or boil for 5–6 hours.
6 Turn out and serve hot with cream, soured cream sauce (page 71) or real custard sauce (page 69).

Roast turkey with chestnut and mushroom stuffing (p. 95), Mince pies (p. 92), Round Christmas pudding with brandy hard sauce (p. 88), Fruity Christmas pinwheels (p. 94)

Rich Mincemeat
Makes 4.5 kg/10 lb

A traditional recipe and well worth trying, but if you would rather tread cautiously at first then make up half quantities. Alternatively, if you would prefer not to add beef at all, then use extra dried fruit instead.

450 g	shredded suet	1 lb
350 g	large seedless raisins	12 oz
350 g	currants	12 oz
250 g	sultanas	8 oz
1	lemon, rind and juice	1
500 g	topside of beef, minced finely twice	1 lb
100 g	flaked almonds	4 oz
350 g	dark soft brown sugar	12 oz
250 g	candied *or* mixed peel, chopped	8 oz
250 g	cooking apples, peeled and grated	8 oz
2.5 ml spoon	ground cloves	½ teaspoon
2.5 ml spoon	cinnamon	½ teaspoon
2.5 ml spoon	ground ginger	½ teaspoon
150 ml	ruby port	¼ pint
150 ml	brandy	¼ pint

Method
1 Put all the ingredients together into a bowl and mix very well together. Cover with cling film and leave in a cool place if possible, though not a fridge, and stir well twice a day for three days.
2 Pot in clean, sterilised cool jam jars and cover with waxed discs and jam pot covers, then seal with metal caps if you still have them. Label and store in a cool, dry place. It will keep for several weeks but once opened, store in the fridge.

Mince Pies Roll out 250 g/8 oz flaky or shortcut pastry to 5 mm/¼ in. thickness. Cut out rounds to fit bun tins with smaller rounds for tops. Fill with mincemeat, cover, glaze and bake at 200°C/400°F/Gas Mark 6 for 20–25 minutes.

Honey Mincemeat

Here are a couple more mincemeat recipes that are perhaps a little less expensive to make and each with a delicious difference.

150 g	shredded suet	6 oz
200 g	currants	8 oz
200 g	apples, peeled and grated	8 oz
100 g	prunes *or* dates, stoned and chopped	4 oz
150 g	raisins	6 oz
200 g	sultanas	8 oz
1	orange, rind and juice	1
150 g	clear honey	6 oz
4 × 15 ml spoons	brandy, optional	4 tablespoons
5 ml spoon	mixed spice	1 teaspoon
2.5 ml spoon	ground nutmeg	½ teaspoon

Method
1 Mix all ingredients together well.
2 Cover and keep cool for two days, stirring often.
3 Pot in clean, sterilised and cool jars.

Lemon Mincemeat

2	large lemons	2
6	apples, peeled and grated	6
225 g	shredded suet	8 oz
500 g	currants	1 lb
250 g	sugar, soft brown *or* granulated	8 oz
100 g	candied *or* mixed peel	4 oz
5 ml spoon	mixed spice	1 teaspoon

Method
1 Peel the lemons and boil the peel until very tender, then mash to a pulp.
2 Add the other ingredients, then squeeze the juice from the lemons and stir this in.
3 Store in a cool place for about two days, stirring occasionally then pot in clean, sterilised cool jars. Allow to stand for a week before using.

Fruity Christmas Pinwheels
Makes about 12

Try these instead of mince pies. The ingredients are the
same but perhaps they have a more attractive presentation, especially for children.

150 g	self-raising flour	6 oz
5 ml spoon	mixed spice	1 teaspoon
75 g	shredded suet	3 oz
1	egg, size 3, beaten	1
225 g	mincemeat	8 oz
	extra beaten egg *or* milk, to glaze	
100 g	icing sugar, sifted	4 oz
	warm water, to mix	
	some chopped glacé cherries, to decorate	

Method
1 Sift the flour with the mixed spice.
2 Mix with the suet and the egg to a firm, soft dough
adding a little milk if necessary.
3 Roll out on a lightly floured board to a large rectangle,
5 mm/¼ in. thick.
4 Spread the mincemeat over the pastry to within 1
cm/½ in. of the edges. Roll up and cut into 1 cm/½ in.
slices.
5 Place these on a greased baking sheet, glaze with extra
beaten egg or milk and bake at 200°C/400°F/Gas Mark 6
for 10–15 minutes or until golden and cooked.
6 Scoop onto a cooling tray to cool. Mix the icing sugar
with just enough warm water to make it the consistency
of thick runny honey.
7 Put a small blob in the centre of each pinwheel and
top with a small piece of cherry. Serve cold.

CHRISTMAS STUFFINGS

A stuffing not only helps a bird to go further, it also
imparts a delicious flavour to the flesh and if it contains a

rich fat, such as suet, helps keep the flesh moist – an important consideration for larger birds which take longer to cook and so can be a little on the dry side. On festive occasions, the bird often has two stuffings, one in the body cavity and one under the neck flap to help keep the shape of the bird. Don't pack the stuffing in too tightly or it will cook in a solid mass. For large birds, rather than trying to fill the body cavity with stuffing, place a couple of peeled onions or a whole lemon in first to bulk it out a bit. Alternatively, you could make little stuffing balls and roast these round the bird for the last half hour of cooking, but then the bird may not be quite as tasty.

Chestnut and Mushroom Stuffing

For medium turkeys and large chickens.

250 g	fresh white breadcrumbs	8 oz
125 g	shredded suet	4 oz
1	onion, chopped finely	1
1–2	cloves garlic, crushed	1–2
100 g	bacon or ham, chopped	4 oz
250 g	fresh, shelled and roasted chestnuts or canned and drained, chopped	8 oz
100 g	mushrooms, chopped	4 oz
2	eggs, size 3, beaten	2
2 × 5 ml spoons	dried marjoram or oregano	2 teaspoons
	salt and ground black pepper	

Method

1 Prepare and clean the bird thoroughly, removing any traces of blood. Wipe the cavity and under the neck flap with a clean kitchen paper towel.

2 Mix up the stuffing and spoon into the chosen end of the bird.

3 If stuffing the neck end, then secure the flap either with fine skewers or sew with fine cotton thread and a trussing needle. For the body cavity, truss the bird well and tie the legs together to contain the stuffing.

Apple and Prune Stuffing
For a small goose or large duck

250 g	dried prunes, soaked overnight	8 oz
2	large cooking apples, peeled and grated	2
1	lemon, rind and juice	1
2	sticks celery, chopped finely	2
1	onion, finely chopped	1
	the bird's liver, chopped	
	a little oil for frying	
100 g	fresh white breadcrumbs	4 oz
75 g	shredded suet	3 oz
5 ml spoon	dried rubbed sage	1 teaspoon
1	egg, size 3, beaten	1
	salt and ground black pepper	

Method
1 Cook the soaked prunes gently in the soaking water for 15 minutes. Drain, reserving the juice, stone and chop the prunes.
2 Prepare the apples and mix with the lemon rind and juice.
3 Fry the celery, onion and chopped liver in a little oil until just cooked.
4 Mix all the ingredients together, adding a little of the prune juice if needed to make a firm but soft mixture.
5 Stuff into the bird as for a turkey (*see* previous recipe).